I0083253

LGBTQ+ HEROES

LGBTQ+ HEROES

51 INSPIRING ICONS WHO CHANGED THE WORLD

A Queer History Book for Kids

L. V. HESTON

ILLUSTRATIONS BY HELDER OLIVEIRA

callisto
publishing
an imprint of Sourcebooks

Copyright © 2025 by Callisto Publishing LLC
Cover and internal design © 2025 by Callisto Publishing LLC
Illustrations by Helder Oliveira
Author photo courtesy of Sarah Miller
Series Designer: Brian Lewis
Art Director: Angela Navarra
Art Producer: Stacey Stambaugh
Editor: Kristen Depken
Production Editor: Rachel Taenzler
Production Designer: Martin Worthington

Callisto Kids and the colophon are registered trademarks of Callisto Publishing LLC.

All rights reserved. No part of this book may be reproduced in any form or by any electronic or mechanical means including information storage and retrieval systems—except in the case of brief quotations embodied in critical articles or reviews—without permission in writing from its publisher, Sourcebooks LLC.

This publication is designed to provide accurate and authoritative information in regard to the subject matter covered. It is sold with the understanding that the publisher is not engaged in rendering legal, accounting, or other professional service. If legal advice or other expert assistance is required, the services of a competent professional person should be sought. —From a Declaration of Principles Jointly Adopted by a Committee of the American Bar Association and a Committee of Publishers and Associations

All brand names and product names used in this book are trademarks, registered trademarks, or trade names of their respective holders. Callisto Publishing is not associated with any product or vendor in this book.

Published by Callisto Publishing LLC C/O Sourcebooks LLC
P.O. Box 4410, Naperville, Illinois 60567-4410
(630) 961-3900
callistopublishing.com

Library of Congress Cataloging-in-Publication Data is on file with the publisher.

This product conforms to all applicable CPSC and CPSIA standards.

Printed in the United States of America

For my brother Tony, my very first LGBTQ+ hero

CONTENTS

INTRODUCTION

What makes a hero? Heroes are people who think beyond themselves. They want to change things not just to improve their own lives, but also to benefit others. **LGBTQ+** heroes in sports, music, and politics might **come out** without knowing if they will be accepted, hoping to make it easier for people who come out after them. Ordinary people become heroes by dedicating their lives to helping fight a deadly disease, creating art that makes people think, or standing up for the things they believe are right. Heroes look around, ask themselves how they can make their community a better place, and then act on it. This book showcases a wide range of LGBTQ+ heroes with different professions, backgrounds, and identities. I hope it teaches you a bit about these 51 heroes and inspires you to find others. There are many more LGBTQ+ heroes out there and, hopefully, more books about them to come.

This book is for everyone, but especially LGBTQ+ youths. It's important to be able to look up to people who are like you. They inspire you and show you what is possible, even when things seem hard. LGBTQ+ books for youth are being banned from schools and libraries across the United States. That this book may be banned in some places is reason enough for it to exist. After all, it found you.

✳ OSCAR WILDE ✳

1854–1900

Oscar Wilde wrote plays, poems, and novels. He was known for his sense of humor and his unique style. His plays are still regularly performed around the world.

Born in Dublin, Ireland, Oscar was the middle of three children. His father was an ear and eye doctor, and his mother was a political poet. The family would vacation in the Irish town of Galway, which was known for its folk music and fairy lore. When Oscar was 13, his little sister Isola died suddenly. He carried a lock of her hair with him for the rest of his life to inspire him to do the things she could not.

At 25, Oscar moved to London and began making a name for himself as a playwright. He also wrote children's stories, essays, and poetry. Oscar's writing was influenced by his time in Galway and, later, his studies of Greek myths. Oscar was put off by the wealthy people in London. He used his sense of humor to show how uptight and silly they could be. His audiences loved it. Oscar became a well-known and well-regarded artist.

Oscar also drew attention with how he looked. He grew his hair long and wore bow ties, hats, and capes, a way of dressing known as the "dandy" style. But, even as a famous artist, he was not free to live as he pleased. Oscar had relationships with men, but because this was not allowed at the time, he was put on trial and sent to prison for two years. When Oscar was released, he left London for Paris, where he lived out the rest of his life. Robert Ross, his former companion and best friend, was with him when he died.

After his death, Oscar's reputation was initially damaged but rose steadily once again. He is now remembered as a literary genius, fashion icon, and challenger of the restrictive customs and laws of his time. His legacy has been strongest for the LGBTQ+ audiences who have enjoyed his work ever since.

> **66** Always forgive
> your enemies;
> nothing annoys
> them so much. **99**

EXPLORE MORE!

The Oscar Wilde Memorial Bookshop opened in 1967 as the first **gay** and **lesbian** bookshop on the East Coast of the United States. Until it closed in 2009 it served as a community gathering space for gay people in New York City and is now considered an important historic site in LGBTQ+ history.

KATHLYN OLIVER

1884–1953

Kathlyn Oliver was a British housekeeper who became an activist fighting for the rights of others.

Kathlyn was born in London to parents who did not have a lot of money. Her father died suddenly when Kathlyn was in her early twenties. This meant that she had to go to work to support herself. Domestic work (cleaning, cooking, and caring for the homes of others) was the only option for an uneducated girl like her. Kathlyn worked for a few families who paid her very little, made her work long hours, and treated her poorly.

Eventually, Kathlyn worked for a family she liked. They helped her pursue her education and political interests. She thought that other workers shouldn't have to rely on the kindness of families for fair treatment. Kathlyn talked to other houseworkers who agreed their work should be well-paid, include breaks, and have shorter hours. They wanted these rules to be looked after by the government to make sure no other families were mistreating their workers. Together, Kathlyn and the other women formed an organization called a trade union. It supported workers' rights.

In her personal life, Kathlyn wanted a romantic relationship with a woman. Since this was not allowed at the time, she placed advertisements in newspapers with hidden messages. Following the example of gay men at the time, Kathlyn described herself as artistic, unconventional, and a "woman bachelor." Other women who loved women would know what she meant when they read these ads.

Kathlyn's organization made working conditions better for men and women houseworkers in the United Kingdom. She felt no one should be mistreated. Along with fair working conditions, Kathlyn believed people should have the right to love whomever they wanted.

> **"** I have been more in love with women than I have with any of the opposite sex... I cannot explain this (perhaps) unnatural state of things, but I know it is so. **"**

EXPLORE MORE!

There have been workers' rights movements in many countries around the world with the goal of improving wages and workplace protections. To learn more about unions, you can watch a short video called "What Are Unions and How Do They Work?" on YouTube. See page 212 for the link.

* ALAN L. HART *

1890–1962

Alan L. Hart was a scientist who discovered a new X-ray technique. He was also the first **transgender**, or **trans**, man in the United States to go through a documented **gender-affirming** medical **transition**.

Alan was born in 1890 in a small town in Kansas. He was **assigned female at birth**, which means that when he was born, the doctors told Alan's parents he was a girl. This was based only on what Alan looked like on the outside, but this is not how Alan ended up feeling inside. Alan identified more as a boy than a girl from a very young age.

Alan's father, Albert, died suddenly from a disease called typhoid fever when Alan was just two years old. Alan went on to be an impressive student, graduating at the top of his classes in high school and medical school. But he never forgot the loss of his father, and he spent much of his professional life researching early detection of disease.

At first, Alan presented as a woman in public but knew he was a man. He asked a doctor he knew to help him affirm his gender through medicine, so he could look more like how he felt. Alan told the doctor he wanted to have his uterus removed because it is a female organ. The doctor agreed, and Alan became the first person in the United States to have his uterus removed for this reason. After the surgery, Alan cut his hair short, wore men's clothing, and started introducing himself as a man. Sometimes people he knew before his transition would threaten to tell his new friends about his past. These threats caused Alan and his wife, Edna, to change jobs and move multiple times. Later in his life, Alan took male hormones to deepen his voice and grow facial hair.

At work, Alan was a cutting-edge researcher on tuberculosis, a lung infection that can be deadly. He realized that doctors could use X-rays of patients' chests to diagnose the illness and begin earlier treatments. His discovery saved thousands of lives!

66 I have been happier since I made this change than I ever have in my life, and I will continue this way as long as I live. **99**

EXPLORE MORE!

Operation Ouch is a YouTube channel with hundreds of videos that explain medical issues to kids. Check out their video "How Do X-Rays Work?" See page 211 for the link.

✳ DOROTHY ARZNER ✳

1897–1979

Dorothy Arzner was a Hollywood film director in the 1920s and 1930s, one of the few women doing that job at the time.

Dorothy grew up in Hollywood, California, where her dad owned a restaurant called the Hoffman Café. Many people working in the movie business would eat there, including some famous directors. That's where Dorothy got her first look at the life she would later lead.

Dorothy started working at a film studio typing scripts. She eventually got the chance to edit a film, which earned her a lot of praise and respect in the industry. She made a case for directing her first feature, *Fashions for Women*, by pointing out that a woman might know better than a man how to direct a movie meant for women viewers. She directed both silent films and "talkies," or movies with sound. Dorothy brought a new perspective to directing that allowed her to show women characters that people didn't see in other movies. These women were strong, complicated, and had important friendships with other women rather than just chasing men.

Well-known actors wouldn't work with Dorothy at first. But Dorothy directed the early work of people who went on to become Hollywood superstars, like Clara Bow, Katharine Hepburn, and Joan Crawford. Dorothy was very private about her personal life, but she had a long-term romantic partner, Marion Morgan. Marion was a dancer and created the dance scenes in several of Dorothy's films.

Over a 15-year career, Dorothy directed more movies than any other American woman in history. The way she presented women in the 1920s helped inspire the strong women leads we see in movies and television today.

> 66 Box office appeal is thought of largely in terms of the women lined up at the ticket window. If there are no women directors, there ought to be. 99

EXPLORE MORE!

Which women characters from movies and television are strong? Take a minute to list as many as you can think of now, or start to pay closer attention to the things you watch in the next few weeks.

GLADYS BENTLEY

1907–1960

Gladys Bentley was a **drag king** and blues singer who performed during the **Harlem Renaissance.**

Born in Philadelphia, Pennsylvania, Gladys was the oldest of four children. Her mother was from Trinidad, and her father was African American. From a young age, Gladys felt more comfortable in boys' clothes and felt like she wanted to date women rather than men. Gladys's parents took her to several doctors to try to "fix" her. She was bullied in school for her size and for dressing like a boy. At 16, Gladys moved from Philadelphia to the neighborhood of Harlem in New York City. There, she found many Black and **queer** people just like her and realized there was nothing wrong with her at all.

Gladys was a very popular performer in Harlem nightclubs. She played piano and sang the blues in a top hat and tuxedo. Some considered the songs she sang "unladylike," but for others that was what made her act something to see. Gladys did not follow the rules and expectations people put on women. One club even had to get special permission to have Gladys perform in pants rather than a skirt or dress.

Gladys was as open about her **sexual orientation** as a woman could be at the time. When she was interviewed by a reporter, Gladys said she was married to a woman. Gladys was always interested in causing a stir, so we're still not sure if it is true.

Gladys's incredible musical talents and bright white suits attracted crowds of admirers at the peak of her career. Not many people knew Gladys's story, but today she is being redis-covered as the icon she always was.

"I have earned the distinction of being the first, and in some cases, the only performer of my race to crash the most plush glitter spots."

EXPLORE MORE!

The Harlem Renaissance of the 1920s and 1930s was a significant period in American history. Black Americans like Langston Hughes, Zora Neale Hurston, Duke Ellington, and Louis Armstrong were establishing new forms of art and living that were all their own.

✳ BAYARD RUSTIN ✳

1912–1987

Bayard Rustin was an American civil rights activist who worked closely with Dr. Martin Luther King Jr. He believed in achieving equality through nonviolent forms of protest.

Born in Pennsylvania, Bayard was raised by his mom and grandparents, all immigrants from Caribbean islands known as the British West Indies. Bayard played football in high school, worked odd jobs, and attended several colleges without graduating. He found his true purpose in activism.

Bayard believed in challenging unfair laws peacefully. To do this, he had to be creative. Bayard was a driving force in several of the most important nonviolent protests in American history. Bayard was a Freedom Rider, which meant he intentionally rode on buses with white people and sat at the front when it was against the law for Black people to do so. Freedom Riders were arrested, but they were successfully calling attention to a law they felt shouldn't exist. When other Americans saw pictures of these protests, their opinions on these laws changed and, eventually, so did the laws.

Bayard also worked very closely with Dr. Martin Luther King Jr. and influenced the belief in peaceful protest he was known for. Bayard was the main organizer of the 1963 March on Washington, DC, where Dr. King gave his famous "I Have a Dream" speech. The people Bayard worked with knew he was gay. Some of Dr. King's other advisors told him he should stop working with Bayard because of his sexual orientation, but Dr. King refused.

For the rest of his life, Bayard fought for justice. He got involved in the movement for workers' rights. He believed the movement for LGBTQ+ rights would be the next struggle for civil rights in the United States. In 2013, well after Bayard's death, President Barack Obama awarded him the Presidential Medal of Freedom. This award is the highest honor a civilian can receive. It was accepted on Bayard's behalf by his life partner, Walter Naegle.

> **"** Let us be enraged about injustice, but let us not be destroyed by it. **"**

EXPLORE MORE!

To learn more about great Black leaders in the American civil rights movement and others, check out the book *Black Heroes: 51 Inspiring People from Ancient Africa to Modern-Day USA* by Arlisha Norwood.

✳ ALAN TURING ✳

1912–1954

Alan Turing was a mathematician and likely the world's first computer scientist. He developed a machine that led to victory over the Nazis in World War II. That same machine became the basis for modern computers.

Alan was born in London and had an older brother, John. Alan's parents couldn't always take care of their two sons, so Alan and John grew up in multiple families' homes. Alan loved chemistry and mathematics from an early age and did not find school to be very challenging. Alan fell in love with the only other boy as smart as he was at school, Christopher Morcom. When Alan was 18, Christopher died suddenly, and Alan was left heartbroken. Alan vowed to continue his studies on behalf of himself and Christopher.

Most people in his day believed there would never be a machine that would be as smart as a human, but Alan proved them wrong. He found that if you give a machine the right instructions, it can complete a task on its own. This thinking is the basis of all computer programs.

Alan's knowledge of computers allowed him to help the United Kingdom during World War II. He worked with a group of people on a top secret project to decode Nazi communications. Alan helped break the code and end the war. But Alan's relationships with men were against British law, and he was punished for them in 1952. Alan died just two years later.

Alan Turing was a genius. He developed new ways to use math, engineering, and logic to solve problems humans couldn't figure out by themselves. We all benefit from Alan's work today every time we use our computers, tablets, and smartphones.

66 I feel sure that I shall meet [Christopher] again somewhere and that there will be some work for us to do together, as I believed there was for us to do here. **99**

EXPLORE MORE!

Science, technology, engineering, and math (STEM) are important subjects for anyone to learn about. Have fun with STEM by finding a local science or hands-on museum near you!

CHAVELA VARGAS

1919–2012

Chavela Vargas was a Costa Rican–Mexican singer famous for singing passionate songs traditionally sung by men to attract women.

Born in Costa Rica, Chavela's parents were unhappy with the way she felt most comfortable dressing: like a boy. They would hide her when people came to visit. Chavela knew she wasn't meant to stay in the shadows—she was meant to sing! As a teenager, Chavela ran away to Mexico City and sang in the streets until she was discovered as a great musical talent.

Chavela sang traditional Mexican songs known as *rancheras*. They were written for men to sing, but Chavela made them her own. These songs were full of emotion, and Chavela sang them like no one had heard before. She made a big impression on the artist Frida Kahlo, with whom she is rumored to have had a love affair. Chavela was said to have had relationships with many famous women in her lifetime, but she did not come out as a lesbian until she was 81. She enjoyed the stories she heard about herself and encouraged the ones she liked, so it is hard to know how much is true.

After a long time away from singing, Chavela made a comeback! Her music found new life in the films of Pedro Almodóvar, a famous Spanish director. Chavela also appeared in the biopic *Frida*, singing one of her most famous songs, "La Llorona." In 2007, Chavela received a lifetime achievement award from the Latin Recording Academy, a huge honor.

Chavela's powerful voice changed the way people thought of Mexican rancheras. By refusing to hide her true self, she made others reconsider who could sing love songs to women.

> **"**I am a friend of life. At 80 life tells me to behave like a woman and not like an old woman.**"**

EXPLORE MORE!

If you have never heard a Mexican ranchera, listen to one now. "La Llorona" is a classic!

✳ JAMES BALDWIN ✳

1924–1987

J ames Baldwin was one of the greatest American writers of the twentieth century and a civil rights activist. His novels and essays are as beautifully written as they are bold.

The eldest of nine children, James was born and raised in New York City. He was raised by his mother and stepfather, a Baptist minister. As a kid, James spent a lot of time in the public library, reading and writing poems and stories. James spent his high school years as a street preacher. This experience helped him think and talk about the more difficult things in life, like losing loved ones and falling on hard times. James worked many odd jobs before becoming a famous writer.

At first, James published book reviews and short pieces in magazines. The novelist Richard Wright helped him get enough money to write his first novel, *Go Tell It on the Mountain*. James was also writing powerful essays about **racism** in America. James's grandfather had been enslaved, and James felt that just freeing enslaved people was not enough to make Black and white people equal in America. Black Americans still faced

discrimination and were more likely to be mistreated, imprisoned, and poor. James got very involved in the civil rights movement for racial equality. He was friends with Malcolm X, Dr. Martin Luther King Jr., and Bayard Rustin.

Even though he was famous, when James wrote a novel about a gay relationship, he had a hard time getting it published. *Giovanni's Room* became a landmark LGBTQ+ novel for adults. James wrote more books after that, some with gay and **bisexual** characters. He was also interviewed on television about the civil rights movement because he was a captivating speaker.

James continues to influence new writers and activists after his death. Recently, he was a central figure in an Oscar-nominated documentary. The film connects his work and legacy to the Black Lives Matter movement. He's also been celebrated as a gay literary icon for not shying away from LGBTQ+ themes and characters.

> **66** Those who say it can't be done are usually interrupted by others doing it. **99**

EXPLORE MORE!

The Lambda Literary Foundation was formed in 1987. Each year dozens of LGBTQ+ books and authors are nominated for the foundation's awards, called Lammys. LGBTQ+ literature has come so far! You can find a list of Lammy-winning books on their website. See page 211 for the link.

MAYBELLE BLAIR

1927–

Maybelle "Mae" Blair was a pitcher in the
All-American Girls Professional Baseball League.
Today, she's fighting for a Women's Baseball Hall
of Fame and recently came out as gay at the age of 95!

Mae was born in California into a family that loved baseball.
When Mae was growing up, her father and brothers played
baseball but only let her keep score. In fifth grade, Mae formed
her own softball team with girls at school, but no one wanted to
practice as much as she did! She kept playing and got very good.
In the 1940s, while she was still in high school, Mae started
playing semiprofessional softball. She soon went professional,
making $60 a week—a good salary back then.

In 1948, Mae got her big break when she was scouted for the
Peoria Redwings, a team in the All-American Girls Professional
Baseball League (AAGPBL). The AAGPBL was created during
World War II because many men's major league players went to
war. It only lasted from 1943 to 1954, but it was made famous
in the 1992 movie *A League of Their Own*. The league had rules
about how players had to dress, on and off the field. They had

to play baseball in skirts and makeup. Mae hated sliding into a base in a skirt. An injury forced Mae out of the league after just one season, but she went back to playing softball for a time. After that, Mae had a long career at a company that made airplanes, becoming one of the only women managers there.

Mae is a big supporter of women's and girls' baseball, and she still attends events and speaks about her experience today. In 2022, at 95 years old, Mae came out publicly as a lesbian, saying it was something she felt she had to keep to herself for over 75 years. Mae's announcement was met with a standing ovation from the crowd.

❝ I have been one of the luckiest people in the whole cockeyed world. ❞

EXPLORE MORE!

You can learn about the league and other women professional baseball players on the AAGPBL's website: aagpbl.org.

HARVEY MILK

1930–1978

Harvey Milk was one of the first openly gay elected officials in U.S. history. Harvey advocated for fairness to members of the LGBTQ+ community and others.

Harvey was born on Long Island, New York. His parents, William and Minerva, were proud of their Lithuanian-Jewish heritage. He and his brother Robert worked at his family's department store, Milk's. In high school, Harvey was popular and enjoyed opera and playing football. He studied math and history in college and wrote for the student paper. His classmates did not suspect Harvey was gay, but he did have relationships with men. After graduation, Harvey enlisted in the Navy. The military banned gay service members, and Harvey was kicked out when he was discovered. Harvey moved to New York City and found community with gay people who were more politically informed and fought for gay rights.

Harvey had various jobs before his time in politics. He was a public school teacher, financial analyst, Broadway production assistant, and owner of a camera store. All these jobs led Harvey to see how the government often failed regular people, especially people who were gay.

Harvey moved to San Francisco in 1972 and quickly began running for local political offices. He failed the first few times, but his message of equality attracted a lot of supporters. Harvey wanted to create daycare centers for working moms, turn abandoned military buildings into affordable housing, and make neighborhoods safer. Harvey was open about being gay and advocating for the rights of other LGBTQ+ people.

In 1977, Harvey won his election to the San Francisco Board of Supervisors. He now had a loud voice people in the local government would listen to. Sadly, within his first year in office, Harvey was **assassinated** by an antigay politician he worked with. People across the country and world held demonstrations in Harvey's honor.

Today, there are many streets, schools, and a foundation named after Harvey Milk. He is remembered as a pioneering gay-rights advocate and icon.

66 All young people, regardless of sexual orientation or identity, deserve a safe and supportive environment in which to achieve their full potential. 99

EXPLORE MORE!

May 22 is Harvey Milk Day in the state of California. The day is to remind people about Harvey's life and his work against LGBTQ+ discrimination.

LORRAINE HANSBERRY

1930–1965

Lorraine Hansberry was a playwright and the first Black woman to have a play produced on Broadway.

Born on Chicago's South Side, Lorraine was the youngest of three children. Her mother was a teacher, and her father founded one of the first banks in Chicago for Black patrons. Lorraine's parents were distinguished members of the Black community. They often hosted prominent Black leaders when they came to Chicago. When she was seven, Lorraine's parents challenged local laws by moving into an all-white neighborhood. When they were forced to leave, they sued the government. In 1940, their case went all the way to the United States Supreme Court, and they won!

Lorraine moved to New York City for school and was drawn to theater and politics. She met her husband, Robert, at a protest. Robert was white, and marriage between Black people and white people was still illegal in many states when they got married. Robert cowrote a famous song that made a lot of money. This gave Lorraine the freedom to focus on writing her play *A Raisin in the Sun*. It was the first play by a Black woman on Broadway, and it was a hit! Themes in the play, like the struggles of low-income Black people in the city, reflected what Lorraine saw during her early life in Chicago. Lorraine's play won many awards, was adapted into several movies, and is now considered a classic.

While married to Robert, Lorraine realized she wanted to be with women instead of men. Robert understood, and after they broke up they remained best friends. Lorraine died of cancer when she was just 34, but Robert published more of her work after her death.

Lorraine's legacy was in writing plays that allowed Black audiences to see theater as a place for them. They were welcome there and could see their experiences reflected on the stage.

66 Never be afraid to sit a while and think. **99**

EXPLORE MORE!

The title of Lorraine's play *A Raisin in the Sun* comes from a Langston Hughes poem called "Harlem: A Dream Deferred." You can hear the poem performed as it is in the play by one of the characters on YouTube. See page 211 for the link.

BRUCE VOELLER

1934–1994

Bruce Voeller was a scientist and gay-rights activist. He was an early researcher of **HIV/AIDS,** a disease that many LGBTQ+ people died from in the 1980s and 1990s before treatments were developed. Bruce cofounded an important rights group to help with the HIV/AIDS crisis.

Bruce was born in Minneapolis, Minnesota, but grew up in rural Oregon. He was an excellent student and athlete, graduating second in his class. From an early age, Bruce knew he was gay. At 15, he confessed his sexual orientation to a minister, who told him to forget about it.

Bruce tried to ignore his feelings. He earned a doctorate in biology. He also married a woman, and they had three children together. But Bruce could not stop feeling what he was feeling. Bruce came out as a gay man at age 29 and divorced his wife. Some people thought Bruce shouldn't be allowed to see his kids anymore because he was gay. Bruce had to fight in court to see his children. His battle went to the Supreme Court and was successful. It helped shape the law for other families that followed.

Coming out had a big impact on Bruce's work as well. There was a new disease killing a lot of gay men in the early 1980s. Bruce used his biology training to study how it spread and who it infected. At first, the name for this disease was "gay-related immune deficiency disease" (GRIDD). Bruce knew that the disease being called "gay" was not only wrong—straight people got it too—but it also made it easier for people to ignore. Bruce renamed the disease "acquired immune deficiency syndrome," or AIDS. He wrote dozens of papers on how the disease spread and how to stop it.

Bruce Voeller's work saved many lives through prevention. It also led to activism to try to change how the government dealt with the disease. Bruce cofounded the National Gay Task Force to focus on that effort and other concerns in the LGBTQ+ community. Its work is still ongoing today, renamed as the National LGBTQ Task Force.

> **"** If I had had the opportunity to know gay people who were open and frank—like those I've known in the movement—it would have changed my life fantastically. **"**

EXPLORE MORE!

Many species in nature exhibit **homosexual** behavior, including apes, lions, wolves, cows, bats, penguins, and other birds. Some even mate with a same-sex partner for life!

✳ LYNN CONWAY ✳

1938–2024

Lynn Conway was a trans woman computer scientist and an engineer. She revolutionized computer microchip technology.

Lynn grew up in and around New York City. She was a curious and adventurous child and had sweet early memories of being with her mom, dad, and little brother. Lynn was **assigned male at birth**, but she knew that she was a girl from around age four. She asked for dresses and told her mom she was a girl. Her mother told Lynn she wasn't a girl and never would be. At 14, Lynn read about Christine Jorgensen in the newspaper. Christine was one of the first women to publicly change genders. This gave Lynn new hope, and she knew science had a big part in Christine's transition.

Lynn got very interested in science and technology. She studied engineering at Columbia University. In 1963, she joined the computer company IBM and helped make computers faster and more powerful. She was building on the invention of another LGBTQ+ hero, Alan Turing, in her own work! In her personal life, Lynn was innovating as well. She began her transition while working at IBM. When her bosses found out, they fired Lynn and did not give her credit for her work.

Lynn went to Europe for her gender-affirming surgeries and returned to the United States as the woman on the outside she always knew she was on the inside. She started a new job and hid her past from her new coworkers. Now that she was happier, Lynn's work took off. She and another computer scientist designed a new computing method that allowed small teams to design powerful computer chips.

Lynn's work changed the way schools taught computer science. She was inducted into the National Inventors Hall of Fame. In the 1990s, Lynn came out publicly as trans to inspire other people who wanted to change their gender and show them they could succeed. In 2020, IBM formally apologized for firing Lynn and honored her with a big award for her work.

> **"If you want to change the future, start living as if you're already there."**

EXPLORE MORE!

Lynn is listed on a website called 500 Queer Scientists (https://500queerscientists.com/). This was made to show just how many LGBTQ+ scientists there are working today and inspire young people to study STEM. There are already way more than 500 scientists' stories there!

✳ ANGELA DAVIS ✳

1944–

Angela Davis is one of the most recognizable civil rights activists of the 1960s and 1970s.

Angela grew up the oldest of four kids in Birmingham, Alabama. Both her parents were teachers. When Angela was four, her family moved to a neighborhood that was mostly white. The neighborhood was nicknamed "Dynamite Hill" because white people bombed houses to try to scare Black people into moving away, but Angela's family didn't move. In high school, Angela was part of an exchange program where she lived with a white family in New York City. There she found people who believed in racial equality.

After witnessing so much discrimination, Angela was committed to **social justice**. She went to Germany to study philosophy with a famous thinker who believed in equality. After earning her PhD, Angela moved to California and started a job as a professor. The university fired her for her political beliefs, which was illegal. She got her job back but became the target of many threats. She was linked to people who tried to break someone out of prison and was wanted by the FBI. Angela was arrested and spent 16 months in prison waiting for her trial. She was found innocent.

Angela saw what life was like in prison and how poorly inmates were treated. It made her think no one should be in prison. Angela is such a good writer and speaker that she is now one of the most famous activists for the rights of people in prison. She's published many books on the topic. People were surprised in 1997 to learn that Angela is a lesbian because it was not a big part of her activism early in life. She came out in an interview with a gay magazine called *Out* because she wanted to bring attention to inequalities faced by LGBTQ+ people.

Angela used her fame from having been on the FBI's list of the ten most wanted fugitives to bring attention to a cause she believed in. She's helped many people see prisoners as humans who deserve rights and fair treatment.

> **"**I am no longer accepting the things I cannot change. I am changing the things I cannot accept.**"**

EXPLORE MORE!

Sometimes books are hard to come by in prisons, but book donations can help. See if your library is taking donations for prisoners and contribute some books you don't need. There is interest for titles for LGBTQ+ people especially.

* MARSHA P. JOHNSON *

1945–1992

Marsha P. Johnson was a leader of the gay and trans rights movement in New York City during and after the **Stonewall Rebellion** of 1969.

Born in New Jersey, Marsha was assigned male at birth. She was the fifth of seven kids and grew up without much. Her dad was a factory worker, and her mom was a housekeeper. At age five, Marsha started wearing girls' clothes and felt more like herself. Other kids bullied her, though, so she stopped for a time. After high school, Marsha moved to New York City with only a bag of clothes and $15.

In New York City, Marsha got to dress and act exactly how she wanted. She was known for her joyous nature and flower crowns. Marsha also got to choose her own name. When asked what the "P." in her name stood for, she would say it meant "pay it no mind," her motto for the hard times in life. Marsha used she/her **pronouns** and identified most with being a **transvestite** or a **drag queen**. This was before people used the term transgender, or trans. Marsha's best friend was Sylvia Rivera, a girl like her.

New York was more accepting of gay and trans people than many places, but some things were still illegal in the 1960s. Men couldn't dance with other men in public. Gay and lesbian bar patrons were often harassed and harmed by the police. On June 28, 1969, police went to the Stonewall Inn, a well-known gay bar, to arrest people for being gay. Instead of going quietly, Marsha, Sylvia, and others fought back. They started a riot that led to protests and demands to have a safe place to be themselves. Each year LGBTQ+ **Pride** Month is in June to commemorate the Stonewall Rebellion, the day people say began the modern gay and lesbian liberation movement.

Marsha and Sylvia's efforts did not end there. They were part of national LGBTQ+ groups and would always advocate that trans people be included. They also started the first organization to protect homeless LGBTQ+ youths in NYC.

> **"** No pride for some of us without liberation for all of us. **"**

EXPLORE MORE!

There are groups and services for LGBTQ+ youths in trouble today, including the Trevor Project, the Ali Forney Center, Casa Valentina, and Haus of Codec.

✳ VITO RUSSO ✳

1946–1990

Vito Russo was a gay-rights and HIV/AIDS activist and film historian who studied LGBTQ+ themes in popular movies.

Vito was born in New York City and grew up with his dad, who worked in construction. Vito liked to read books. He knew he was gay from a young age but never felt there was anything wrong with it. He lived in New Jersey for high school and college, but Vito knew he belonged in Manhattan because it had an exciting gay culture that he wanted to be part of.

In 1969, Vito witnessed the Stonewall Rebellion. After that, he got very involved in activism, joining the Gay Activists Alliance (GAA), which fought discrimination in New York City. Vito loved movies and ran public screenings of his favorite movies for the GAA. He decided to study film at New York University.

Vito wrote a book about the history of gay people in movies. Gay characters were often used as jokes or villains and always seemed to die tragically on screen. This did not reflect Vito's life as a gay man. He and his friends would joke and laugh and experience heartbreak and disappointment. In real life, he was just as complex as any straight person, and he wanted gay characters in film to be the same.

To that end, he cofounded GLAAD, an organization that promotes better images of LGBTQ+ people in all forms of media, including books, movies, and television. Vito was also living with AIDS at a time when most people were ignoring it. He knew that the way the general (straight) public saw gay people was more important than ever before. Vito cofounded ACT UP, a group that brought attention to the AIDS crisis and the importance of getting the government to help find a cure. Vito's life was dedicated to activism. Through the organizations he started and the legacy he left, that work continues in his name.

> **"** Hollywood is too busy trying to make old formulas hit the jackpot again to see the future. Hollywood is yesterday, forever catching up with what's happening today. **"**

EXPLORE MORE!

The Vito Russo Test is a way to shed light on how LGBTQ+ characters on a TV series or movie are portrayed. There are three questions in the test: (1) Is there an LGBTQ+ character? (2) Is the character's LGBTQ+ identity the only thing you learn about them? And (3) Does the LGBTQ+ character "matter" to the overall story? What have you seen that passes the test?

* HOWARD ASHMAN *

1950–1991

Howard Ashman was an accomplished musician who wrote the lyrics for some of Disney's best-known songs.

Howard grew up in Baltimore, Maryland, in a house filled with music. He loved theater from a young age, writing and directing original musicals for his little sister's birthday parties. Howard started performing in local theater when he was just six years old.

In college, Howard majored in theater, focusing on directing and writing. He worked for a book publisher before returning to his love of theater in New York City. In the late 1970s, Howard met his friend and lifelong collaborator Alan Menken. They started working on musicals together. Alan wrote the melodies, and Howard wrote the words. Their first big hit was *Little Shop of Horrors*. It won many awards, became a movie, and is still popular today.

Howard and Alan's biggest successes came when they started working for Disney. Together, Howard and Alan wrote the songs for *The Little Mermaid*. They treated the film like a musical. This new approach was a huge success for Disney, whose animation department had been failing. Howard and Alan won an Academy Award for the song "Under the Sea." After that, Howard and Alan wrote the songs for *Beauty and the Beast* and won another Academy Award! Unfortunately, Howard became sick with AIDS while working on his final Disney movie, *Aladdin*, and sadly passed away. Disney dedicated *Beauty and the Beast* to him, saying, "To our friend, Howard, who gave a mermaid her voice and a beast his soul, we will be forever grateful."

Howard was openly gay while creating some of the most iconic songs in the history of animation. His work is kept alive playing in homes and on stages—and at Disneyland, of course.

> 66 **In almost every musical ever...the leading lady sits down on something and sings about what she wants in life. And the audience falls in love with her and then roots for her to get it for the rest of the night.** 99

EXPLORE MORE!

Has it been a while since you watched one of the movies Howard worked on? Watch them again and really listen to the lyrics he wrote. Do you think the words he wrote for a mermaid, genie, or beast were sometimes really about himself?

✳ SALLY RIDE ✳

1951–2012

Sally Ride was a physicist and astronaut for NASA. She was the first American woman to go to space.

Sally grew up in Los Angeles and was a big sister to Karen, whom she nicknamed Bear. Sally's dad was an Army veteran and schoolteacher. Her mom was a homemaker and an activist for women's prison reform. Sally was always quiet. In school she liked math and science classes best. Outside of school, Sally was nationally ranked as a junior tennis player.

Science was Sally's true passion. Instead of pursuing a tennis career, she got a doctorate in astrophysics. Sally became an astronaut by reading the newspaper. She saw an ad that said NASA was looking for new astronauts and applied. Most astronauts were former military pilots—and always men. For the first time, both men and women could apply. Out of 8,000 applications, Sally was chosen as one of 35 people in the new astronaut class. NASA liked that Sally was an athlete. It showed she was committed, strong, and calm under pressure.

In 1983, Sally was chosen to become the first American woman to travel to space. She knew there would be a lot of attention on her. Reporters asked her **sexist** questions like, "Do you cry when things don't go right?" and "Do you plan to have a baby?" The men on her crew were never asked things like that.

Sally went to space on two separate missions and said it was the most fun of her life. She was married to a man, a fellow astronaut, from 1982 to 1987. When her marriage ended, Sally started a relationship with a woman. Sally was in a long-term relationship with a friend from her tennis days, Tam O'Shaughnessy, for 27 years! After her career at NASA ended, Sally and Tam started Sally Ride Science, an organization that encourages women and girls to pursue careers in science and technology.

> **" All adventures, especially into new territory, are scary. "**

EXPLORE MORE!

Sally and Tam wrote a series of science books for kids, including *Mission: Planet Earth* and *Mission: Save the Planet*. These books introduce climate change science to young people and suggest things we can all be doing to fight global warming and preserve the planet.

✳ BEN BARRES ✳

1954–2017

Ben Barres was a scientist who studied brains and disease. He was transgender and encouraged women and trans people to get more interested in science and math.

Born in West Orange, New Jersey, Ben was assigned female at birth. He was raised with three sisters, including a twin. Ben's dad sold baby furniture and his mom was a homemaker. As early as five years old, Ben knew two things: he wanted to be a scientist, and he was a boy. Ben didn't feel like he could tell anyone he was transgender, so he lived as a girl until much later.

Ben was drawn to science and math in school. When he was growing up, girls were not always allowed to take advanced science classes. Even when Ben proved to be an impressive student in college, he had trouble finding mentors who'd work with a scientist like him, who they saw as a girl. Ben still succeeded and became a professor at Stanford University in California. As a neuroscientist, he studied what others thought were unimportant brain cells, called glial cells. Glial cells were considered useless "packing peanuts" of the brain. While the brain's nerves got all the attention, Ben was sure that the glial cells weren't just there to hold the nerves in place. He ran experiments in his lab and proved he was right! His findings have helped doctors find potential cures for brain diseases.

Ben did not come out as trans until he was 40 years old. He was really worried about what his students and colleagues would think, but they were very supportive. After that, many young LGBTQ+ scientists asked Ben for his advice. He encouraged them all to live openly as themselves sooner than he did. He also encouraged women to enter science careers. He knew the value of people who were once overlooked in science, just like the humble glial cells were!

> **“** I am happy to be an openly transgender scientist and to serve as a role model for young LGBT scientists. I hope that I have helped ease their way a little bit. **”**

EXPLORE MORE!

Are you interested in learning more about how brains work? *Frontiers for Young Minds* is an online science magazine for kids. Their site has articles on the brain like "How Does the Brain Help us Understand Others?" See page 211 for the link.

✳ SVANTE PÄÄBO ✳

1955–

Svante Pääbo won a Nobel Prize in medicine in 2022. He is a bisexual Swedish scientist who studies human evolution.

Svante was born and raised in Stockholm, Sweden. Both his parents were scientists. His dad, Sune Bergström, won a Nobel Prize in 1982 for his work in biochemistry. His mother, Karin, encouraged Svante's scientific interests and helped him believe in himself. Svante loved the idea of discovering things no one had seen before, like the tombs that once held Egyptian kings. Svante would pretend to be an Egyptologist, digging around in forests in Sweden, looking for mummies and buried treasure. His mom even took him on a trip to Egypt to see the pyramids in person.

Svante ended up studying medicine instead of Egyptology, but he was still fascinated by ancient things. As a student, he thought we might be able to extract DNA (genetic information) from mummies found in Egyptian tombs and other preserved ancient bodies around the world. He was afraid his advisor would think it was silly and not support him. Most scientists thought it was impossible. But after many years of trying, Svante did it! This technique helped him discover a new kind of hominid, an extinct ancient human, using a single finger bone found in Siberia!

Svante identified as a gay man when he went to teach in Berkeley, California. There he met a woman graduate student named Linda who rode a motorcycle to the lab every day. Meeting Linda and finding her attractive made Svante realize that he was bisexual. He liked Linda's "boyish charms" so much that he married her. Svante has been openly bisexual ever since.

With the DNA technique Svante established, we now know a lot more about our evolutionary ancestors and can study what makes us different from them and from one another. During the COVID-19 pandemic, Svante's work showed how some people's DNA made them more likely to get a bad case of the virus.

" DNA is the blueprint for our biology and the history of our species. **"**

EXPLORE MORE!

To learn more about evolution, visit a museum of natural history near you. You can see how other species change over time and get a look at models of extinct human species like the Neanderthals.

FÉLIX GONZÁLEZ-TORRES

1957–1996

Félix González-Torres was a gay Cuban American artist. He was known for the sculptures he made using everyday objects.

Born in Guáimaro, Cuba, Félix grew up as one of four children. At age seven, Félix got his first set of paints from his dad. When he was 14, there was a war happening in Cuba. Félix's parents sent him and one of his sisters to Spain to keep them safe. After that, they moved to Puerto Rico and lived with their uncle. In time, the rest of the family moved to Puerto Rico as well.

Félix moved to New York City and studied art and photography. He met his life partner, Ross, a few years later at a gay bar. The two quickly fell in love, moved in together, and shared four cats and a dog. In 1991, they found out Ross was sick with HIV, the virus that causes AIDS. To raise Ross's spirits, Félix would go to garage sales and thrift shops looking for toys to bring him. He especially liked big, colorful plastic cartoon figures.

Félix expressed himself with art. He wanted people to interact with the things he made. Félix's most famous artworks were dedicated to Ross. One was a billboard in New York City that was just an image of Félix and Ross's empty bed that looked like it had just been slept in. Another was a pile of individually wrapped candies, often swept into a corner in a museum. The pile started out each day at 175 pounds, the same amount Ross weighed when he was healthy. It gradually got smaller when people took the candy away with them. This symbolized the weight Ross lost when he was sick. People taking the candy with them spread the art, which was meant to symbolize the spread of the virus itself.

Félix became famous for the activism in his artwork. His pieces helped people understand the HIV/AIDS crisis in a different way. He made it personal for them.

> **"The wonderful thing about life and love, is that sometimes the way things turn out is so unexpected."**

EXPLORE MORE!

Art isn't just painting or sculpture. It comes in many forms. Félix made art with everyday objects like lights, candy, stacks of paper, and clocks. Using them in unfamiliar ways to communicate a feeling made them art. Try it!

✳ SIMON NKOLI ✳

1957–1998

Simon Nkoli was a South African activist. He helped organize the first South African Pride and develop the country's new constitution.

Simon was born in Soweto, South Africa, during a time when Black people and white people were forced to live separately. This was known as apartheid. Even though white people were the minority, they controlled the government and would not allow Black people to have equal rights. Black people did not have voting rights or basic work protections. White people restricted where Black people could live and whom they could marry.

Simon was one of four children and was raised by his grandparents. They wanted him to quit school to work on their farm. He ran away to live with his mom and stepdad, who supported his education. At 18, Simon told his parents he was gay. They tried to "cure" him using religion. When that did not work, they sent him to counseling. Luckily, his counselor was gay and encouraged Simon to live as himself.

Simon joined activist organizations fighting for equal rights. The anti-apartheid group he joined did not like that he was gay, and the gay-rights group he joined did not want to fight for racial equality. To Simon, these were equally important parts of himself. In 1984, Simon was imprisoned for his beliefs that all people should be equal. For four years he secretly sent letters to his lover, Roy, from prison.

After his release, Simon kept fighting for what he believed. He organized the first South African Pride, which protested discrimination and hate crimes against LGBTQ+ South Africans. He also met with a leader of the anti-apartheid movement, Nelson Mandela. Simon's belief in the equality of everyone had a big impact when apartheid was overturned and Nelson became president. Not only did the new South African constitution guarantee rights for Black South Africans, but it was also the first constitution in the world to make gay marriage legal.

> **"In South Africa I am oppressed because I am a Black man, and I am oppressed because I am gay. So, when I fight for my freedom, I must fight against both oppressors."**

EXPLORE MORE!

In 2015, the United States Supreme Court ruled that LGBTQ+ people could marry each other. This was 21 years after South Africa made it legal. Now there are many countries around the world that allow gay people to marry.

✳ KEITH HARING ✳

1958–1990

Keith Haring was a famous artist who drew in a signature cartoon graffiti style. He wanted his art to be seen by everyone, so he put it on billboards, subway cars, and T-shirts.

Born in Reading, Pennsylvania, Keith had three younger sisters who also had K-names: Kay, Karen, and Kristen. Keith was interested in art from a young age, and his dad taught him how to draw.

Keith initially went to art school but left early. He spent some time traveling to see a band called the Grateful Dead. He would sell shirts with his art on them at their shows. He had his first art show at just 19 years old in Pittsburgh. A year later, he moved to the place he would call home for the rest of his life: New York City. There he made friends in the art and LGBTQ+ communities. Keith thought art was for everyone, not just museums. He drew inside subway cars and graffitied blank walls. It's illegal to do this without permission, so Keith was arrested a few times. Keith's art was already so popular that police officers arresting him would ask for his autograph! Keith's art touched on a lot of political themes, including AIDS awareness and messages against South African apartheid.

Keith opened a store to sell his art called Pop Shop. He printed his drawings on T-shirts, posters, and socks, and sold them cheap so even kids could afford them. Across town, his paintings were selling for thousands of dollars at a gallery. In 1986, Keith was hired to do a giant 10-story mural of the Statue of Liberty. He asked hundreds of high school students to finish it with him, and they did. Sadly, Keith contracted HIV and died when he was just 31.

Keith's art is very simple and can be appreciated by anyone. In his short life, Keith produced a lot of work that you can still see in museums around the world and printed on T-shirts sold today.

> **"** I am interested in making art that can be experienced and understood by everyone. **"**

EXPLORE MORE!

You would probably recognize Keith's art if you saw it. He drew simple and colorful images of people and animals. Try creating your own Keith Haring–inspired drawings.

✳ ALISON BECHDEL ✳

1960–

Alison Bechdel is a cartoonist and graphic memoirist. One of her graphic memoirs, *Fun Home*, was turned into a popular Broadway musical.

Alison was born in a small farm town in Pennsylvania. She grew up as the middle child between two brothers. As a kid, Alison had short hair and carried a pocketknife with her. Her parents were both schoolteachers, but her dad, Bruce, also worked as a part-time funeral director. The kids spent a lot of time with him in the funeral home, which they jokingly called the "fun home."

Alison always loved art. She started drawing cartoons at age three and kept a detailed journal. She would make daily entries noting what happened to her and the thoughts she had. Alison went to college in Ohio to study art and art history. In college, she realized she is a lesbian and wrote a letter to her parents about it. Her dad called to congratulate and support her, but her mom didn't want to speak to her. Soon after, Alison's dad died suddenly. Alison's mom started talking to her again. In fact, she told her an important and surprising piece of information: Alison's dad, Bruce, had been a gay man living **in the closet** all his life. This was hard for Alison's mom.

After college, Alison struggled to find her place. She found a book of gay comics that gave her an idea. Alison wanted to write about young lesbians like her. At 23, she published her first comic in a newspaper. She started her own comic strip after that. It showed the life of LGBTQ+ people in America and was a huge success. It ran every week in newspapers across the country for 15 years!

Alison wrote a graphic memoir about growing up in the funeral home, her dad, and her own coming-out story. She called it *Fun Home*. It was a huge hit! It was adapted into a Broadway musical and won five Tony awards (the highest honor for theater), including Best Musical in 2015. Now, Alison lives a quiet life teaching and drawing comics in Vermont.

"Autobiographical comics, I love them. I love them.**"**

EXPLORE MORE!

Before the Vito Russo film test for gay characters, there was the Bechdel test for women. This began as just a line in Alison's comic, but now it's in gender studies books everywhere. To pass the test, a movie has to have three things: (1) two or more women must be in it, (2) they have to talk to each other, and (3) they have to talk about something other than a man. Do you know any movies that pass this test?

☀ GREG LOUGANIS ☀

1960–

Greg Louganis is a diver who won four Olympic gold medals. He's widely considered to be the greatest diver of all time.

Greg was born in San Diego, California, and adopted when he was nine months old. In school, Greg was teased for his learning differences and Samoan heritage. He threw himself into sports. Greg's first love was gymnastics, but he also danced and swam. Greg started diving competitively at age ten and did very well.

In 1976, at just 16 years old, Greg went to his first Olympic Games. He won a silver medal in springboard diving. In 1980, the USA team boycotted the games in Russia, so he could not compete. But in the next summer Olympics, in 1984, Greg won gold medals in both springboard and platform diving. No one had done that for 56 years!

In the 1988 Olympics, Greg competed in both events again. During a practice dive, Greg hit his head on the board and suffered a concussion. The crowd was shocked! He knew people would understand if he quit and that his friends and family would still love him. But, after four stitches and 35 minutes of rest, Greg was back on the board. His next dive was flawless. Greg walked away with another two gold medals. He's the only man to ever win gold in both diving categories in two Olympic Games in a row.

After his diving career ended, Greg became an actor and model. In 1995, Greg came out as both gay and HIV-positive in a TV interview with Oprah Winfrey. Greg was already out to his family, friends, and teammates, but he wanted to be out to the public before his autobiography *Breaking the Surface* was released. Greg sometimes struggled on the diving board and off, but his persistence kept him doing the things he loves. In addition to acting and writing books, Greg works with charities to raise awareness about HIV and promote LGBTQ+ rights.

66 Fear is a part of everything you do... You have to take great risks to get big rewards. 99

EXPLORE MORE!

Greg showed the importance of cross-training. His gymnastics and dance background made him especially graceful in his dives. Many professional football players do ballet or dance to improve their strength, speed, and balance.

✳ WILLI NINJA ✳

1961–2006

Willi Ninja was a dancer and choreographer in the New York City **drag ball** scene.

Willi was born in Flushing, Queens, in New York City. He learned to dance at a young age, and his mom often took him to the ballet and other dance performances. Willi knew he was gay but never had to come out to his mom. She told him she just knew and was very supportive. Willi's gay peers were often kicked out of their homes and cut off from their families. Willi wanted to give these people the chance to have the kind of support his mother had given him.

While attending beauty school in Manhattan, Willi got very involved in an LGBTQ+ performance scene known as **ballroom**. Ballroom performances happened mostly in secret clubs. There, LGBTQ+ people could live and socialize freely, though they were often intimidated by police. The clubs were especially important spaces for people of color who were battling racism and felt excluded from the white gay community.

In the drag ball scene, Willi met many young people who no longer spoke with their families. He and others organized "houses" that acted as **chosen families** for people who needed them. They helped and supported each other when no one else would. To express themselves, house members would compete in events like dancing, singing, and modeling. Willi founded the House of Ninja, known for its dance moves. Willi specialized in voguing: quick, sharp dance movements that combine posing with gymnastic martial arts. He made it into a popular art form and taught it to the pop singer Madonna.

Willi and other **drag mothers** became known to the wider public through a 1990 documentary about them called *Paris Is Burning*. It showed their lives on and off the stage. Willi is known as the Grandfather of Vogue. Though he passed away from AIDS in 2006, his house still has over 200 members and people are still voguing in gay clubs today.

"Voguing is about embracing who you are and celebrating your uniqueness. It's a form of self-expression and empowerment."

EXPLORE MORE!

Willi inspired a Google Doodle, celebrating his life and work. Clicking on it leads to a short video that shows what voguing looks like. See page 211 for the link.

✳ RUPAUL CHARLES ✳

1960–

RuPaul is a host, singer, and the world's most famous drag queen. His reality-competition show, *RuPaul's Drag Race*, has launched the careers of hundreds more.

RuPaul Andre Charles (known simply as RuPaul or Ru) was born in San Diego, California. He grew up with his mom and three sisters. Before Ru was born, a fortune teller told his mom that her son would grow up to be a star. Ru liked to sing, dance, and act in plays. He did not fit in with the other boys at school. They would make fun of Ru for seeming more like a girl than a boy.

Ru was not the best student. He skipped so many classes that he got expelled from school once. When he was 15, Ru moved to Atlanta, Georgia, with his sister and her husband. There he studied theater at an art school that was a much better fit. Ru moved to New York City in 1987. Ru has always identified as a man, but his drag persona is a glamorous woman. Ru wears big wigs and colorful designer dresses and bodysuits.

It didn't take too long for Ru to become a star after all. In 1992, he released his first single, "Supermodel (You Better Work)," which became a surprise hit. In 1994, Ru became the very first face of the M·A·C makeup brand. But Ru's career reached new heights after he started hosting *RuPaul's Drag Race* in 2009. He went from an LGBTQ+ icon to a household name. Ru is the show's host and a mentor for all the queens who compete to be American's next drag superstar. Ru now has 14 Emmy Awards for hosting the show, the most any person of color has ever received.

Over a long career, Ru has acted in over 50 movies and TV shows and released 18 music albums. He has a wax double (in drag) in Madame Tussauds wax museum and a star on the Hollywood Walk of Fame.

> **"We're all born naked, and the rest is drag."**

EXPLORE MORE!

Have you ever seen a drag queen in real life? Some libraries and bookstores have events like drag queen story hour where you can meet a drag performer and hear them read a kids' book.

CAROLYN BERTOZZI

1966–

Carolyn Bertozzi is a queer scientist who won a Nobel Prize in Chemistry in 2022. Her work helps diagnose and treat diseases.

Carolyn was born in Boston, Massachusetts, the second of three daughters. Her parents met at the Massachusetts Institute of Technology, where her dad was a professor and her mom was a secretary. Carolyn's parents taught their three girls that education was very important. Carolyn was afraid to come home with less than an A on any test because the punishment would be sitting down with her father to go over and over the questions until she got them right. Math always came easily to Carolyn's older sister, a math genius, but it took Carolyn a little longer to find her way.

Carolyn was recruited to play soccer at Harvard University, but she stopped playing as soon as she got there to focus on her studies. She began as a biology major but loved chemistry so much that she switched. There were only a few other women chemistry majors back then. Carolyn became so passionate about chemistry that she went to graduate school and became a professor of it. One of Carolyn's big accomplishments is developing a whole new chemistry subfield: bioorthogonal chemistry.

Chemistry is the study of what makes up all the things in the universe. These bits, or elements, can be combined to make chemical reactions, which means you can combine two elements to make something we already know about or create something totally new.

Carolyn's work helps people by using chemical shortcuts that speed up the time it takes to develop new treatments for cancer, COVID-19, and other illnesses. Carolyn's parents taught her how important education is. Her own experience showed her it can be harder to succeed when you are trying to do something that few people like you are doing. She now passes these lessons on to her students, along with teaching them cutting-edge chemistry that saves lives.

66 If you learned something from it, it's not a failure. 99

It can be hard to picture a chemical reaction. We put salt on roads during the winter to melt ice into water faster. There are also chemical reactions when we combine ingredients to make a cake, which is why the batter seems to grow from being heated. Can you think of other examples of chemistry in action?

* ANDERSON COOPER *

1967–

Anderson Cooper is an award-winning journalist and news anchor. He has written several books and regularly cohosts *New Year's Eve Live*.

Anderson was born into a prominent New York family. His mother, Gloria Vanderbilt, was a railway heiress, actress, model, and founder of her own brand of designer jeans. His father, Wyatt Cooper, was an actor and writer. Wyatt died when Anderson was ten years old, which was very difficult.

Anderson knew that people thought he didn't need to work hard to succeed because of his family name, connections, and wealth. This made him even more determined to make a mark. Anderson studied political science at Yale University. After college, he worked as a fact-checker for Channel One News. Wanting to be closer to the news itself, Anderson took a video camera to the Southeast Asian country Myanmar (formerly Burma), where there was a lot of political unrest. Channel One then made him their chief international correspondent.

Anderson has been a reporter for ABC and CNN. He's won many awards as a news host, including 18 Emmys!

Anderson thought that being openly gay would negatively impact his career. In 2012, at age 45, he came out publicly as a gay man. He realized that not coming out gave the impression he was ashamed, which he wasn't. The next year, GLAAD awarded him their Vito Russo Award for accelerating LGBTQ+ acceptance in media. In 2020, Anderson did something unusual. He became a parent with his ex-partner, Benjamin. While their romantic relationship did not work out, they stayed good friends and still wanted to become parents together. As someone who grew up with only one parent, Anderson wanted as much love in his son's life as possible. As a gay man, he knew the value of chosen family and making the kind of family you want. He named his son Wyatt, after his own dad. In 2022, Anderson and Benjamin had a second son, Sebastian.

> **"The fact is, I'm gay, always have been, always will be, and I couldn't be any more happy, comfortable with myself, and proud."**

EXPLORE MORE!

Is there something or someone in your life you want to learn more about? Anderson would tell you to talk to people who know more and to ask them questions. Try interviewing someone you'd like to know more about and really listen to what they have to say.

QUEEN LATIFAH

1970–

Queen Latifah is a Grammy-winning rapper and Academy Award–nominated actor. She is the first woman rapper to get a star on the Hollywood Walk of Fame.

Queen Latifah was born Dana Elaine Owens in Newark, New Jersey. Her dad was a police officer, and her mom was a schoolteacher. When she was eight, a cousin gave her the nickname Latifah, which means "delicate and sensitive" in Arabic. She sang in the church choir as a kid and had an early interest in acting.

In high school, Latifah became Queen Latifah when she started rapping with an all-girl group of rappers called Ladies Fresh. In 1988, at age 18, Queen Latifah signed a recording contract as a solo artist. As her music career was taking off, Queen Latifah also started acting in movies. As an actor, Queen Latifah is known for her comedic ability and her sensitive demeanor. She was a core cast member on a comedy series called *Living Single* in the 1990s. It is still one of only a few comedies to focus on the lives of Black women.

In 1996, she portrayed a lesbian bank robber in *Set It Off*, which sparked rumors that she might be a lesbian. When asked, Queen Latifah would say she wanted to keep her personal life private but was not insulted by people thinking she was gay. In 2003, Queen Latifah was nominated for an Academy Award for Best Supporting Actress when she played another queer character, Matron "Mama" Morton, in the film version of the musical *Chicago*. She's the only woman rapper in history nominated for an acting Oscar.

After being famous for several decades, it was a big deal when Queen Latifah officially came out as part of the LGBTQ+ community. She confirmed it in an acceptance speech when she won BET's 2021 Lifetime Achievement Award. She thanked her long-term partner Eboni Nichols and their child, Rebel. Because it was June, she also wished everyone happy Pride.

> **"Look at people for an example, but then make sure to do things your way. Surround yourself with positive people."**

EXPLORE MORE!

Queen Latifah has been nominated for several Nickelodeon Kids' Choice Awards over the years. This is the only awards show where kids decide who they like best in music, film, and TV. You can vote on the latest award nominations on their website. See page 211 for the link.

* LAVERNE COX *

1972–

Laverne Cox is an actress, producer, and trans-rights advocate. She is the first trans woman to be nominated for an Emmy.

Laverne and her twin brother, M Lamar, were born in Mobile, Alabama. Their mother was a schoolteacher. Laverne was assigned male at birth and raised as a boy. She was a very creative child and loved performing. Laverne took dance classes but got bullied for being girly.

Laverne found a more supportive community through the arts. She went to a fine arts high school and college to study dance. She entered college as a **gender-nonconforming** person. She knew she was a woman but was afraid of what being trans would mean for her life. There were a lot of myths and misunderstandings about transgender people in television and movies. Trans characters always seemed to be sad and tragic.

When she transferred to a college in New York City, Laverne met trans people who were happy and successful. Laverne found the courage to come out as trans. She also shifted her artistic focus toward acting. In 2007, Laverne saw something that changed everything for her career. Candis Cayne, a trans actress, had a big role in a television show, and Laverne realized she could do that too. And she did! In 2012, Laverne got her big break on the Netflix series *Orange Is the New Black*.

Laverne's success has inspired many more trans and gender-nonconforming actors to pursue their passions. She has used her platform to advocate for trans civil rights and appeared on the cover of *TIME Magazine* in 2013, when much of America was just learning what it meant for a person to be trans. Laverne wanted to make sure they understood the truth about trans people: that they are real people. To that end, she also produced a documentary, *Disclosure*, which showed how trans characters and roles change the way trans people are seen in society.

> ❝ My life changed when I realized I deserve to be seen, to dream, to be fully included, always striving to bring my full humanity. ❞

EXPLORE MORE!

Laverne is a Barbie! Mattel honored Laverne as part of their Tribute Collection by making a collectible Barbie that looks just like her. Mattel says they did this because "Laverne Cox uses her voice to amplify the message of moving beyond societal expectations to live more authentically."

✳ THOMAS BEATIE ✳

1974–

Thomas Beatie is a trans activist and public speaker. He became famous on a television talk show in 2008 and was known globally as "the pregnant man."

Thomas was born and raised in Honolulu, Hawaii, and assigned female at birth. His mother was a special education teacher, and his dad was a contractor. Sadly, Thomas's mother died suddenly when he was 12. Thomas was a **tomboy** and never liked wearing women's clothes. As a teen he was kicked out of women's restrooms because people thought he was a boy. He competed in karate and tae kwon do competitions and won.

In his 20s, Thomas was a competitive bodybuilder and met his first wife, Nancy, while he still identified as a woman. Thomas started taking testosterone, a hormone that makes people appear more masculine, around 2001. By 2005, he'd received **top surgery**, updated the **gender marker** on his identification, and moved to Oregon with Nancy. Thomas had always wanted to become a parent. Even though he was a man, he kept his uterus so he might carry a baby someday. Other trans men had become pregnant and had children before, but when Thomas was pregnant in 2008, he became a media sensation called the "world's first pregnant man."

Thomas wanted people to know that he and Nancy were doing what so many other couples do—they were just doing it a bit differently. Thomas and Nancy faced a lot of difficulties at doctors' offices and were denied treatment, disrespected, and laughed at many times. They went on a popular television show in part to raise awareness so it would be easier for any pregnant trans men after them.

Today, Thomas is a father of four kids. He's a stockbroker in Arizona and living a relatively quiet life. He showed the world that not only did some trans men want to become parents, but they could also use their own bodies to do it and still be men.

> **"Different is normal and love makes a family. And that's all that matters."**

EXPLORE MORE!

Media literacy is an important skill to have. It helps us understand the difference between fact and fiction when we see and hear news stories. It also helps us think deeper about things some people take for granted. A YouTube video for kids called "What Is Media Literacy?" can help you learn more. See page 212 for the link.

✳ JASON COLLINS ✳

1978–

Jason Collins played in the National Basketball Association (NBA) for 13 seasons. He made history as the first out gay player in a major American men's sport.

Jason was born in Northridge, California. His parents thought they were having only one child when Jason was born. Jason had a surprise twin, Jarron! Growing up, Jason's parents gave their sons an appreciation of history, art, and Motown music.

Jason knew he was attracted to boys since he was in junior high. He says when Jarron first showed interest in girls, they started to fall out of sync as twins. On the outside, the brothers were still very connected. Jason and Jarron played basketball together in school, winning two state titles. They attended Stanford University together and played basketball there. They were even drafted into the NBA together in 2001, Jason going to the New Jersey Nets and Jarron to the Utah Jazz.

Jason was known as a physical defender. He says he preferred that role; rather than being the star, he helped his teammates shine. As the center, he went up against some of the NBA's all-time greats, like Shaquille O'Neal.

In the last years of his career, Jason wore number 98 to commemorate the 1998 murder of Matthew Shepard, a young man in Wyoming who was killed for being gay. It was Jason's secret nod to the LGBTQ+ rights movement. Jason did not want his coming out to negatively impact his teammates, so he waited until 2012 when he was a free agent (not attached to any team). He came out in a story he wrote for *Sports Illustrated*. Though the response was mostly positive, Jason had to wait many months before a team asked him to play. When he rejoined the Nets, his teammates were very supportive. No other NBA player has come out, even after Jason paved the way. But when they do, it will be a little easier because of him.

> **66** There's nothing more beautiful than just allowing yourself to really be happy and be comfortable in your own skin. **99**

EXPLORE MORE!

The Trevor Project was founded in 1998 after the death of Matthew Shepard. The organization provides support specifically for LGBTQ+ youths. There are many resources available on their website: thetrevorproject.org.

✳ CHE FLORES ✳

1979–

Che Flores is a referee in the NBA. They are the first out trans and **nonbinary** ref in a professional American sport.

Che (pronounced like "shay") was born in Los Angeles, California. They were assigned female at birth and grew up as the eldest of three in a predominantly Mexican American neighborhood. Their mother is Costa Rican, and their father is Mexican American. Che grew up playing sports and was called a tomboy. Their mother played in a softball league with lesbians. It seemed to Che that the only two choices were to be a feminine girl or a more masculine lesbian, and neither felt right for them.

Che always loved basketball and was a star player in high school and college. They did not really like the referees at their own games. Che would sometimes get into arguments about a call with the ref. It hadn't occurred to them to become one! But their dad was refereeing high school games and told them to try it out. They were also inspired when they saw Violet Palmer, the first woman NBA ref, who showed that the job wasn't just for men.

Before becoming the first nonbinary referee in the NBA, Che spent a decade refereeing for NCAA (college basketball), NBA G League (minor league basketball), and WNBA (women's professional basketball). Each league had their own rule book, but Che was exceptional at their job and always remembered to enforce the right rules.

When they were promoted to the NBA in 2022, they were not yet out as nonbinary. The announcement congratulated them for being a new woman ref, but that wasn't who Che really was. In 2023, they changed their pronouns to they/them and their name at work. They knew how important it was for someone on a national stage to be visible as a queer person and show LGBTQ+ youth what is possible.

> **"I have a community of people [and] I want them to know that someone like them exists."**

EXPLORE MORE!

We can't all be professional athletes, but there are plenty of other jobs you can get that are essential to bringing pro competitions to life and keep you close to a game you love. There are not only refs and coaches but also physical therapists, sports agents, commentators, journalists, camerapeople, facilities managers... And the list goes on!

* ORLANDO CRUZ *

1981–

Orlando Cruz is a Puerto Rican boxer who competed in the 2000 Summer Olympic Games in Sydney. He came out as gay in 2012 and remains the only professional men's boxer who has come out as LGBTQ+.

Orlando was born in Yabucoa, Puerto Rico. He was always fighting, even in his earliest school days. Orlando's mom, Dominga, brought him to a boxing gym so he could channel his need to fight and learn the discipline to control it. He knew from a young age that he was gay, but when he was growing up, the worst thing you could call a boy was gay. It was considered an insult at the time.

After 12 years of boxing, Orlando got the opportunity to represent Puerto Rico at the 2000 Olympic Games. Though he did not win a medal, he was extremely proud of having made it that far. When he returned to Puerto Rico, he started boxing professionally. Orlando won 25 bouts in his career and lost just 7.

In 2012, just ahead of one of the biggest fights of his career, Orlando came out as a gay man. He says the response was 95 percent supportive and he ignores the other 5. Orlando felt much lighter being able to finally tell the truth about who he was. Heading into the world featherweight championship, Orlando dedicated the fight to Emile Griffith. Emile was one of the greatest boxers in history, winning many titles in the 1960s. He also had relationships with men he could never talk about publicly. Orlando says he was lucky to have the support Emile never had. He lost the match, but two months later he married his husband, who always makes him feel like a winner.

Orlando broke a barrier by being the first out men's boxer. In 2013, he was inducted into the National Gay and Lesbian Sports Hall of Fame alongside Greg Louganis, Jason Collins, and other athletes.

" If I am inside or outside the ring, I just want to be me. And now, I'm happy I can do it. I can be true to myself. **"**

EXPLORE MORE!

Gayandlesbiansports.com is a resource that tracks the latest accomplishments by LGBTQ+ athletes. The site also reports on recent attempts to restrict the inclusion of LGBTQ+, especially trans and non-binary, athletes in sports and competition in the United States.

✳ PETE BUTTIGIEG ✳

1982–

In 2020, Pete Buttigieg made history as the first openly gay United States presidential candidate for a major party. He's also the first LGBTQ+ person to serve in the U.S. cabinet.

Pete was born and raised in South Bend, Indiana. Both his parents were professors. Pete grew up as an only child and was very focused on his studies. Even in middle school, people said he should become a politician. To write his speech for eighth grade graduation, he read political speeches delivered by former President John F. Kennedy. To get over his shyness, Pete joined the drama club in high school and continued to be at the top of his class.

Pete went to Harvard University and the University of Oxford. He started getting involved in politics and worked for people running for president. In 2007, Pete enlisted in the military and became a U.S. Navy Reserve officer. Since reservists hold normal jobs, Pete pursued his career in politics. He was elected mayor of South Bend in 2011. In 2014, he had to pause his term in office when he was sent to Afghanistan for seven months with the Navy. When he returned, Pete wanted the people of South Bend to know the real him, so he came out as a gay man. This didn't matter to voters, and Pete was reelected mayor in 2015. That same year, Pete met the man who would become his husband, Chasten. After his second term as mayor, Pete ran for president. Unable to pronounce his last name (BOOT-edge-edge), his supporters called him "Mayor Pete."

Though Pete was not nominated for president in 2020, he still made history as the first gay man to get that far. He was chosen for another job by President Joe Biden, who named him Secretary of Transportation. This means Pete was entrusted to run a whole department of the U.S. government. He's the first LGBTQ+ person to hold an office that high.

> **"The most moving responses I got to my coming out...was people, like teenagers, letting me know that it made their lives easier in some way."**

EXPLORE MORE!

Mayors, presidents, secretaries, oh my! If you want to learn more about the United States government, Britannica Kids has an excellent article about the different roles of government and what they do. See page 211 for the link.

✳ LAUREN ESPOSITO ✳

1982–

Lauren Esposito is a scientist who studies scorpions. She's also an activist who started the website 500 Queer Scientists.

Lauren was born in El Paso, Texas. Lauren and her little sister were very involved in Girl Scouts. Both her parents are biologists. As far back as she can remember, Lauren was interested in animals. She'd turn over rocks looking for insects to collect and study later. Her family would visit the Bahamas, where her grandparents lived. There, Lauren would explore and find creatures she'd never seen before.

Lauren went to college early, at age 16. She had a summer internship in arachnology, the study of spiders and scorpions, at the Museum of Natural History in New York City. After that, she knew she wanted to focus on scorpions. Lauren has made a career studying scorpions. As one of the only women in the field, she is known as the "Scorpion Queen"!

Lauren feels that scorpions have a bad reputation. They have stingers, and their armored shells look scary, but she loves them. Scorpions were on the planet before the dinosaurs and look mostly the same today. There are over 2,500 kinds of scorpions and more still to find. They give birth instead of laying eggs, and some of them glow in the dark! Scorpions can be found just about anywhere, and very few are dangerous to humans.

Today, Lauren is the curator of arachnology at the California Academy of Sciences. Even though the museum is based in San Francisco, California, a place with a high population of LGBTQ+ people, Lauren felt lonely as a queer scientist. She knew there were more like her, so in 2018 she started a website to increase the **visibility** of LGBTQ+ scientists. She called the site 500 Queer Scientists in hopes of getting that many stories from scientists across the world. There are now close to 2,000 stories! Lauren hopes that if LGBTQ+ kids see many working scientists who identify as LGBTQ+, more of them will study science too and feel less lonely.

> **66** Innovation is how we make progress and diversity is what's going to breed new ideas. **99**

EXPLORE MORE!

Lauren and others talk about scorpions in a video called "Anomalies: Venom Race" that can be found on YouTube. See page 211 for the link.

* MEGAN RAPINOE *

1985–

Megan Rapinoe is considered one of the greatest soccer players of all time.

Megan was born in Redding, California. She's the youngest of six kids—even her twin sister, Rachael, was born 11 minutes before her! When they were in elementary school, Megan and Rachael played for a boys' soccer team because there were none for girls nearby. In high school, Megan played soccer and basketball and ran track. Megan is a crafty soccer player known for quick shifts that throw opponents off their game. She went to the University of Portland on a soccer scholarship and helped the school win a championship.

Megan played on the U.S. Women's National Team beginning in 2006 as well as for club teams around the world. Megan was cocaptain of the U.S. women's team when they won their second World Cup with her in 2019. Megan received the Golden Boot award (for scoring the most goals in that tournament) and the Golden Ball award (most valuable player of the season) and was named FIFA's Women's World Player of the Year.

Megan is also an advocate for LGBTQ+ rights, women's rights, and racial justice. Megan came out publicly as queer ahead of the Olympic Games in 2012, where the U.S. team took home a gold medal. Despite their success, the U.S. Women's National Team were not making as much money as the players on the U.S. men's team. Megan thought that was wrong. She and some other players sued the U.S. Soccer Federation. Now men and women are paid an equal rate in all soccer tournaments, including the World Cup. For her activism, President Joe Biden awarded Megan the Presidential Medal of Freedom; this is the highest honor someone who is not in the military can get.

At the 2016 Olympics in Brazil, Megan met Sue Bird, a WNBA player on the women's U.S. basketball team. They started dating shortly after and got engaged in 2020. In 2023, Megan retired from soccer, but she continues to use her fame and platform to promote social justice.

> **"Politics is gonna engage with you whether you engage with it or not."**

EXPLORE MORE!

Megan joined Sue in the WNBA's 2020 isolation zone (known as the "Wubble") during the worst of the COVID-19 pandemic, when the league played a condensed 2020 season. While in the Wubble, Megan got a tattoo on her hand ("mammers," a nickname for her mom) from a multitalented referee also isolating there—Che Flores!

✳ JANELLE MONÁE ✳

1985–

Janelle Monáe is a Grammy-nominated musician and award-winning actor. They are an advocate for racial justice, gender equality, and LGBTQ+ rights.

Janelle was born in Kansas City, Kansas. Janelle's mom was a janitor and house cleaner, and their dad drove a garbage truck. Their dad was not around much, so Janelle and their sister, Kimmy, were raised by their mom and grandmother. Janelle credits their mom's sacrifices for giving them the opportunity to succeed. From their grandmother, Janelle learned generosity, forgiveness, and unconditional love. Their grandmother opened her home to anyone who needed it. Some people even stole from her, but she forgave them for it.

Janelle grew up wanting to be a singer and actor. They sang in the church choir and acted in local productions of musicals. They also wrote several plays and musicals before they even got to high school. After high school, Janelle moved to New York City for drama school but did not like the structure. Janelle wanted to write their own musicals, not perform someone else's! They moved to Atlanta and worked at Office Depot while they wrote and recorded songs. They performed and promoted their music on college campuses until they were discovered at an open-mic night in 2005. Big Boi from a hip-hop group called OutKast was in the audience. Just a year later, he put Janelle on two songs on OutKast's album *Idlewild*. Janelle then got their own contract with Bad Boy Records.

Today, Janelle is a celebrated artist. They've been nominated for ten Grammys. They began acting in movies, including *Moonlight*, which won the Oscar for Best Picture in 2017, and *Hidden Figures*, for which they won a Screen Actors Guild Award. In interviews, they came out as nonbinary and said they use they/them pronouns. They are an outspoken advocate for LGBTQ+ causes as well as racial and gender justice. To honor their parents, Janelle has often worn black and white "uniforms" in their performances, just like their parents did at their jobs.

> **66** We come in peace, but we mean business. And to those who would dare try to silence us, we offer two words: time's up. **99**

EXPLORE MORE!

Did you know Janelle once wrote and performed a song for *Sesame Street*? It's called "The Power of Yet," and you can watch the video on YouTube. See page 212 for the link.

* KALI REIS *

1986–

Kali Reis is a women's professional boxer and actor. Kali is part of the Seaconke Wampanoag tribe and an activist for Indigenous Peoples' rights.

Kali was born in Providence, Rhode Island, and is the youngest of five kids. Kali is half Indigenous and half Cape Verdean (Cape Verde is an island nation in West Africa). Growing up, she felt like she did not fully fit in to either community. Kali was in the marching band and color guard and played basketball, volleyball, and softball in school. Kali was a good student, maintaining As and Bs, but she was also the class clown and constantly in trouble.

Kali learned discipline through boxing. When she was 15, a family friend and local Indigenous pro fighter taught her the basics. Kali joined a boxing gym and started competing. At 21, she won major amateur boxing competitions. In the ring, Kali fights using the name "KO Mequinonoag." KO stands for "knockout," a quick way to beat your opponent in a fight. Mequinonoag is the name Kali's mother gave her. It means "many feathers" to honor Kali's numerous talents. Kali went on to win an astonishing six world titles in boxing. She made history by participating in the first ever women's boxing match to air on HBO.

Kali identifies as **Two-Spirit**. This is a gender identity claimed by some Indigenous people. The exact meaning can be different for different people. For Kali it means that she identifies both as masculine and feminine in different contexts. Kali is also open about having had relationships with men and women.

Kali has recently started acting in TV and movies. As a boxer and actor, Kali advocates for Indigenous Peoples. She's most invested in raising awareness of Missing and Murdered Indigenous Women (MMIW). This phrase is used to describe crimes against Indigenous women that are unsolved or haven't been investigated. This is more likely to happen to Indigenous women than any other group of people in the United States. Kali is a fierce fighter in the ring and out.

> **"I fight for us. It's not about me, it's about we."**

EXPLORE MORE!

If you want to know more about the history and current lives of Indigenous Peoples in America, check out the book *Native Americans in History: A Native American History Book for Kids* by Jimmy Beason.

✳ ELLIOT PAGE ✳

1987–

Elliot Page has acted in TV and film for over two decades. He's been nominated for an Oscar and is a *New York Times* bestselling author.

Elliot was born in Halifax, Nova Scotia, Canada. He was assigned female at birth. Elliot's father was a graphic designer, and his mother was an elementary school teacher. Elliot was interested in acting from a young age. He performed in local theater before being cast in a TV movie, *Pit Pony*, at ten years old. He won an award for it! Elliot's been a working actor ever since. Before coming out as trans, Elliot always played characters who identified as women.

After moving to Los Angeles, Elliot had a role in two X-Men movies. His big break came in 2007 with the film *Juno*, where he played a pregnant teenage girl. Elliot was nominated for an Academy Award for the role. With more success came more attention. Elliot was told to wear dresses to events and always felt uncomfortable. When he wanted to come out as LGBTQ+, his agent and others told him it would be bad for his career, so he waited.

In 2014, Elliot attended a conference for the Human Rights Campaign (HRC), an organization that fights for LGBTQ+ rights. He came out as gay in a speech and received a lot of support. Elliot still felt unhappy and like he wasn't truly himself yet. He came out as transgender in late 2020. He changed his name and his appearance. Elliot instantly became the most famous trans man in the world when he came out, though he also identifies as non-binary. He said he was surprised by the response he got, both supportive and not.

Elliot has used this attention to become a public speaker and advocate for the trans community. For Elliot, it has been important to focus on the joy he's felt since coming out. Elliot says that being able to live as himself is more important than anything, even being in movies.

> **66** We deserve to experience love fully, equally, without shame and without compromise. **99**

EXPLORE MORE!

Elliot made an LGBTQ+ travel show with his friend Ian called *Gaycation*. In just ten episodes, the two friends explore LGBTQ+ culture in many places, including Japan, Brazil, Ukraine, and the Deep South in the United States.

* MICHAEL SAM *

1990–

Michael Sam is the first out LGBTQ+ person to be drafted into the National Football League (NFL).

Michael was born in Galveston, Texas. He was the seventh of eight kids. Michael's family experienced a lot of tragedy during his childhood. One of his older brothers was killed, and another has been missing since 1998. Two more of Michael's brothers have been in and out of prison since eighth grade.

Michael started out as a water boy for his high school varsity football team, but he eventually made it onto the squad. Michael excelled in multiple positions, but his mother did not approve of football. It made Michael happy, though, so he often stayed at friends' houses so he could keep playing.

Michael's football talents got him scholarship offers from multiple colleges. He chose the University of Missouri. Michael played very well in college. He was named an All-American all four years, meaning he was judged to be one of the best college players in the country each year. Experts predicted he would be drafted into the NFL as one of the first few players picked.

Michael came out publicly ahead of the 2014 draft, attracting a lot of media attention. Michael fell in expert rankings because people thought no team would take a chance on him. He was drafted in the final round to the St. Louis Rams, the 249th pick of 256 players. Michael was thrilled and kissed his boyfriend Vito on camera to celebrate. Michael only got to play in the preseason before being cut. He was very upset and felt that he had been discriminated against for being gay. After the NFL, Michael spent some time playing pro football in Canada and made history as the first LGBTQ+ player in the Canadian league.

Though Michael never got to play a regular season game in the NFL, he still made history. Jason Collins congratulated Michael when he came out. Like in the NBA, it is still very rare for NFL players to come out as LGBTQ+.

> **"There will always be haters. Small heroes can change society every day. It just takes time."**

EXPLORE MORE!

Michael was also on *Dancing with the Stars (DWTS)*! This show and other reality shows have given LGBTQ+ celebrities a second chance at stardom. Other LGBTQ+ *DWTS* contestants include JoJo Siwa, Jason Mraz, and Jonathan Bennett.

* BOWEN YANG *

1990–

Bowen Yang is the first Chinese American cast member on *Saturday Night Live (SNL)*. His writing and acting on *SNL* have made the comedy show more inclusive for LGBTQ+ people.

Bowen was born in Brisbane, Australia. Bowen's parents are from China and had his sister there. China used to have a policy that parents could only have one child per family, so they moved to Australia to have Bowen. The family moved to Canada when he was still a baby, then moved to Colorado when he was nine.

As a kid, Bowen liked watching late-night comedians and going to comedy festivals. In high school, Bowen joined a comedy troupe. Bowen was voted the member of his class "Most Likely to Be a Cast Member on *Saturday Night Live*," but he didn't think much of it. Around the same time, Bowen's parents read an open chat window on his computer and learned he was gay. They were very upset and sent him to **conversion therapy** sessions. Conversion therapy is an attempt to convince someone they are not really LGBTQ+. It has been proven to be ineffective and harmful. It did not work, and Bowen had to come out to his family again. They are now supportive and proud of him.

Bowen went to college in New York City. He studied medicine and chemistry at New York University but still did comedy on the side. After graduating, he decided not to become a doctor. In 2018, he got a job writing for *SNL* and the next year joined the cast on the show. He's been nominated for Emmys for writing and acting on *SNL*.

Bowen brought a new perspective to the show as the first Chinese American and one of the first out gay cast members. The writing on the show has been even more inclusive of LGBTQ+ voices since he joined. Bowen's fame has grown, and he's appeared in movies and TV shows. Bowen also cohosts the podcast *Las Culturistas* with his friend Matt Rogers.

> **"I'm just a comedian. I don't have all the answers. But I'm not just looking for them online. I'm looking around me."**

EXPLORE MORE!

There are programs all over for kids and teens who want to learn about comedy and performance. You can take online classes in improv and the science of what makes jokes funny via OutSchool. This organization is welcoming and inclusive of LGBTQ+ aspiring comedians. See page 211 for the link.

GUS KENWORTHY

1991–

Gus Kenworthy is a British American freestyle skier and Olympic silver medalist. He's also an actor, model, and mental health advocate.

Gus was born in Chelmsford, England, and grew up with two older brothers. The family moved to the United States when Gus was two. The three boys grew up skiing in Telluride, Colorado. Since age five, Gus knew he was gay. He also knew that none of the boys he skied with thought being gay was cool. They used the word "gay" as one of their most frequent insults.

Gus did not just want to be a good skier, he wanted to be the best. He was not a downhill or cross-country skier—rather, Gus was doing huge jumps and freestyle half-pipe tricks, more like a snowboarder. Gus was known for being fearless and trying new jumps and tricks before anyone else. By 16, he had his first sponsor and started skiing professionally.

Gus competed in the 2014 Winter Olympic Games in Sochi, Russia. He won a silver medal in freestyle skiing, but that's not what got him the most attention. He became known as the American who adopted a family of stray dogs off the streets of Russia and brought them home with him. A year later, he made headlines again by coming out as gay. Gus qualified for the 2018 Winter Olympics in Pyeongchang. This time he got to compete as an LGBTQ+ athlete, making history as the first, along with Adam Rippon, an American figure skater. Before one of his events, Gus kissed his boyfriend Matt on live TV, which became international news.

In 2019, Gus participated in a 550-mile bike ride from San Francisco to Los Angeles called the AIDS/LifeCycle. He and his team raised $250,000 in donations to help fund HIV/AIDS education and prevention. Gus works with other LGBTQ+ charitable organizations to address mental health issues, homelessness, and bullying and harassment in schools.

66 That's definitely not something I had as a kid. I never saw a gay athlete kissing their boyfriend at the Olympics. I think if I had, it would've made it easier for me. **99**

EXPLORE MORE!

Gus works with GLSEN (glsen.org), an organization created in 1990 by a group of teachers with the goal of creating better school environments for LGBTQ+ kids. They help support teachers and students through initiatives like Ally Week, Safe Schools, and Gender and Sexuality Alliances (GSAs).

ALOK VAID-MENON

1991–

Alok Vaid-Menon is a nonbinary poet, performance artist, comedian, model, actor, and fashion designer.

ALOK, as they prefer to be known, was born and raised in College Station, Texas. ALOK's father grew up in Malaysia and moved to India, where he met ALOK's mother. They moved to Texas in 1986 and had ALOK's older sister, Alka, and then ALOK. Most people in College Station were white and conservative. They did not make ALOK's immigrant family feel welcome. The Indian community there was not accepting of gay or trans people, so ALOK did not feel welcome there either. At home, ALOK felt safer. They dressed up in colorful saris (traditional Indian garments for women) with their sister and mother and learned that clothes can make you feel powerful and more like yourself.

ALOK attended Stanford University for college and then moved to New York City, where they found other people like them. ALOK is gender-nonconforming. Although they prefer to wear dresses and skirts and other clothing considered feminine, they also often have short hair on their head and facial and body hair. This is how ALOK feels most like themself. While many trans people want to appear as a man or a woman, ALOK is nonbinary and incorporates aspects of both. This has gotten them a lot of attention.

ALOK has taken their experiences of being a gender-nonconforming, nonbinary trans person and made it the subject of their art and expression. Through their work as a writer, comedian, and model, they raise awareness of people like them and assert that they are equally part of the LGBTQ+ community, even if they are often overlooked.

Today, ALOK's comedy shows are often sold out. They have appeared in a comedy show on Netflix and a TV series. There is a documentary made about them called *ALOK*, and they have won many awards for their contributions to culture and entertainment, frequently being called a trailblazer.

> **"I don't really care about what other people see when they see me. I care about what _I_ see when I see me."**

EXPLORE MORE!

A lot of clothing stores are separated into men's and women's sections. But, as ALOK shows us, people can wear whatever clothes they want. Companies like The Phluid Project create and sell clothes that are **gender-neutral**. They are designed for anyone to wear, regardless of gender.

☀ SAM SMITH ☀

1992–

Sam Smith is a Grammy- and Oscar-winning singer-songwriter. They are the first nonbinary artist to hold the number one spot on Billboard's Hot 100 song chart.

Sam was born in London, England, but grew up in Cambridgeshire. Their father was a truck driver and grocer, and their mom was a banker. Sam identified as gay from age ten. Their parents supported them in their LGBTQ+ identity and singing career from a young age. Sam started out in musical theater and performed with Youth Music Theatre UK. Around this time, Sam says they were going to school in women's clothing, a full face of makeup, and fake eyelashes. They incorporated heels, leggings, and fur coats into their wardrobe.

When they turned 18, Sam moved to London to pursue their singing career. In 2014, Sam released their own album, *In the Lonely Hour*. Sam came out publicly as gay just after the album was released. They said the songs were written about a man who had broken Sam's heart by not returning their affections. Sam turned this sadness into gold—the album was a hit! They received four Grammys for it. The same year, Sam was asked to write and sing the theme song for the latest James Bond film, *Spectre*. That song, "Writing's on the Wall" won the Oscar for Best Song.

In 2017, Sam came out as **genderqueer**, saying they felt as much a man as a woman. Since 2019, Sam has identified as nonbinary and uses they/them pronouns. On Instagram they wrote, "After a lifetime of being at war with my gender I've decided to embrace myself for who I am, inside and out." In 2022, Sam's song with Kim Petras, "Unholy," reached number one on the Billboard Top 100 song chart. It was the most popular song for four weeks! This made Sam the first nonbinary person to have achieved this and made Kim Petras the first trans woman to do the same.

> 66 **When I write sad songs, I feel like I'm sewing up a scar in me, and the outcome always feels so much better than when I write happy ones.** 99

EXPLORE MORE!

Sam has a new podcast where they interview other famous LGBTQ+ people about their early lives and how they found their place in the world. It's called *The Pink House* after their childhood house, which was pink!

* ERIKA HILTON *

1992–

Erika Hilton is a politician and activist for Black and LGBTQ+ rights in Brazil. She is the first transgender person to be elected to the Brazilian parliament.

Erika was born in Brazil and grew up surrounded by strong women. She was assigned male at birth but knew she was a girl. This upset Erika's mother, who was very religious. She sent Erika to live with her uncles in the city of São Paulo. They forced her to go to church, thinking that God would heal the "evil" making Erika believe she was a girl. It didn't work. At 15, Erika was kicked out of her uncles' house and became homeless. She found shelter with other trans women. After six years, Erika reconnected with her mother, who had become more supportive. She moved back home and attended college to study teaching. There, Erika engaged with student politics. She was an activist who would hang posters, march, and shout for change.

In 2015, Erika got into a public fight with a bus company. They refused to use her **chosen name** on her ticket. Erika started a petition that got a lot of attention online. The bus company change their policy. Erika saw something she thought

189

was wrong and fixed it for herself and for the many others who wanted to use their chosen names. She didn't want to stop there.

In 2020, Erika became the first trans person elected to the São Paulo city council. São Paulo is not just the largest city in Brazil, but it is also the largest city in South America. In that role she fought for the rights of women, LGBTQ+ people, and poor people struggling to afford a place to live, like she once did.

Erika now fights for Brazilians on a bigger stage. She was elected to the National Congress of Brazil in 2022.

> **"Even with all this fear, I understand that my presence, as a young Black trans woman from the margins, in the halls of power is also a response to this moment, a demonstration that the social bases are not taking the attacks we've experienced lying down."**

EXPLORE MORE!

Erika used her personal experiences as motivation for the kind of change she wants to see in her country. If you were a politician, what would you fight for?

* LIL NAS X *

1999–

Lil Nas X is a Grammy-winning singer-songwriter. He is known for his bold fashion and status as an LGBTQ+ artist. He was born Montero Lamar Hill in Lithia Springs, Georgia.

Montero grew up with seven brothers and sisters. Though Montero knew he was gay from the time he was five, he grew up in a religious household and attended church regularly. He was afraid to come out because of the bullying and **homophobia** he saw toward LGBTQ+ people.

Montero was quiet in high school but had a second life online as a Nicki Minaj superfan. He was very active on Twitter and had a large following. He would post funny memes and learned how to engage his audience. He started making music under the name "Lil Nas X." "Nas" came from his internet handle (after the rapper by the same name), "Lil" is a word a lot of rappers put in front of their names, and "X" is the Roman numeral for the number ten: the number of years he thought it would take him to get famous. It only took a year. Montero had just started making music when, in 2019, he purchased a beat for

$30 online and sang the lyrics to "Old Town Road" over it. The song was a hit! People loved the combination of country and rap music. "Old Town Road" spent 19 weeks in the number one spot on the Billboard Top 100 songs chart, a new record.

While the song was still popular, Montero came out as gay to his family and fans. He was worried about how people would react. It was June—Pride Month—and he was inspired by all the rainbow flags and LGBTQ+ people looking happy. He said his brother, who is bisexual, helped him come out as well. Since then, Montero has rapidly become an LGBTQ+ icon. He's embraced his gay identity in his music and public persona.

> **66** Live your life to its fullest potential and don't really care too much about what other people think of you. **99**

Some think of Lil Nas X as the first Black cowboy because of "Old Town Road." But Black cowboys have been around since at least the nineteenth century. In 1878, the first motion picture ever made was called *The Horse in Motion*. It featured a Black rider galloping on horseback. You can see it on YouTube and other websites.

∗ GAVIN GRIMM ∗

1999–

Gavin Grimm is a trans-rights activist. Gavin sued his school board for banning him from using the boys' bathroom at his high school and won his case.

Gavin was born in Gloucester, Virginia, and assigned female at birth. Gavin always knew he was a boy. At 14, Gavin came out as trans. With the support of his parents, Gavin told the school principal that he had changed his name, wanted to use he/him pronouns, and asked to use the boys' bathrooms. The principal agreed to all of it. For months, Gavin was able to use the bathroom that matched his gender identity. Then, in 2014, the parents of Gavin's classmates found out. Some of them were mad and went to the school board, which sets policies for all the schools in a district. Gavin attended a school board meeting about him. During this meeting, the parents of his classmates called him "confused" and a "freak" and **misgendered** Gavin in front of him. This was all because Gavin wanted to be able to use the bathroom like any other boy.

The school board passed a policy that forced students to use the bathroom that matched the gender they were assigned at birth. They told Gavin he could use a single, separate unisex bathroom at the school. This singled Gavin out and made him feel unwelcome. Gavin took his case to the American Civil Liberties Union (ACLU), an organization that fights for civil rights. They sued Gavin's school board because the policy they created violated Gavin's constitutional rights. Gavin won his case, which has helped trans students in several states.

Gavin did not plan to be an activist at such a young age, but he could not stay silent. Gavin is now a trans-rights advocate and writer. He was listed as one of *TIME Magazine*'s most influential people of 2017 when he was just 16 years old.

66 If I had a diversity of experiences to learn about in my bookshelf I wouldn't have felt so alone or so unheard. **99**

EXPLORE MORE!

Gavin wrote a book! It's a children's picture book autobiography of his life and experience called *If You're a Kid Like Gavin*. Look for it in your local library.

✳ BILLIE EILISH ✳

2001–

Billie Eilish is a Grammy- and Academy Award–winning singer-songwriter. Billie has used her platform and success to advocate for mental health care, body positivity, and addressing climate change.

Billie's full name is Billie Eilish Pirate Baird O'Connell. She was born and raised in Los Angeles, California. Her older brother, Finneas, added the "Pirate" to her name when she was born. Billie and Finneas's parents were both actors. They home-schooled Billie and Finneas and encouraged them to explore their interests outside school, especially in the arts. Billie grew up singing, dancing, and playing instruments. There was a rule in their house that you didn't have to go to bed if you were playing music. Billie was raised vegetarian but became vegan at age 12 because of her love for animals.

At 13, Billie became famous online for singing a song her brother wrote called "Ocean Eyes." They kept working together, writing and producing songs with very little special equipment in Finneas's small bedroom. That was where they wrote and recorded Billie's hit album *When We All Fall Asleep, Where Do*

We Go? When it was released in 2019, it won five Grammys, including Album of the Year and Song of the Year for "Bad Guy." Billie and Finneas also wrote songs for movies. They won Oscars for Best Original Song twice: in 2021 for the James Bond theme "No Time to Die" and again in 2023 for "What Was I Made For?" from the *Barbie* movie.

Billie officially came out as part of the LGBTQ+ community in 2023 almost by accident. She said she was surprised people didn't already know. She'd never said outright that she is attracted to women, but she also did not think it should be a big deal. Since then, Billie has embraced being part of the LGBTQ+ community in her songwriting.

> **❝I've always done whatever I want and always been exactly who I am.❞**

EXPLORE MORE!

Billie is part of a mental health awareness campaign called "Seize the Awkward" (seizetheawkward.org). The goal is to make it normal to talk to friends about your mental health and ask them about theirs. Just listening to a friend talk about a struggle can make a big difference.

MORE INSPIRING PEOPLE TO EXPLORE

FRIDA KAHLO (1907–1954) was a Mexican painter known for her self-portraits and iconic brow. Her work is mostly in a colorful folk-art style with surrealist elements.

ALVIN AILEY (1931–1989) was a dancer, director, choreographer, and activist. He founded the Alvin Ailey American Dance Theater in 1958 to further the careers of Black dancers.

AUDRE LORDE (1934–1992) was a writer famous for her memoir, essays, and poetry as well as for being an outspoken feminist and civil rights activist.

ERNESTINE ECKSTEIN (1941–1992) was an LGBTQ+ leader fighting for LGBTQ+ equality before Stonewall. She was notable for being the only African American woman at these early protests.

BILLIE JEAN KING (1943–) is one of the greatest tennis players of all time. BJK (as she's known) won 39 Grand Slam titles over a 30-year career and fought for pay equity in the sport.

MISS MAJOR GRIFFIN-GRACY (1946–) has been an activist and organizer for trans rights for over 50 years. Miss Major was at the Stonewall Rebellion and today organizes retreats for trans leaders.

ELTON JOHN (1947–) is an acclaimed British singer, songwriter, and pianist. He has an Emmy, five Grammys, two Academy Awards, and a Tony Award. He is one of only 21 people to have won all four awards.

GILBERT BAKER (1951–2017) was an American artist, designer, and activist. Gilbert designed the very first rainbow LGBTQ+ pride flag in 1978.

SYLVIA RIVERA (1951–2002) was a veteran of the Stonewall Rebellion and an activist for gay and trans rights. She was a community organizer, especially for LGBTQ+ homeless youths in New York City.

LOU SULLIVAN (1951–1991) was an American author and activist known for his work on behalf of trans men. He was one of the first out trans men to publicly identify as gay.

LANA AND LILLY WACHOWSKI (1965– , 1967–) are trans siblings who direct and write for film and television. Most famously, they are the minds behind *The Matrix* film franchise.

MARGARET CHO (1968–) is a Korean American actress and stand-up comedian. Since the 1990s she has been very open about her bisexuality and is an advocate for the LGBTQ+ community.

JANET MOCK (1983–) is an award-winning writer, television producer, and trans rights activist. Her memoir *Redefining Realness* was a *New York Times* bestseller.

DANICA ROEM (1984–) is a Virginia state senator who, in 2018, became the first out trans person elected to a state legislature in U.S. history. Danica is a fierce advocate for the rights of trans kids.

CHELLA MAN (1998–) is an actor, model, artist, jewelry and clothing designer, YouTuber, and LGBTQ+ activist. Chella is a deaf trans man who played mute superhero Jericho in the DC series *Titans*.

GLOSSARY

ASSASSINATED: killed for political reasons

ASSIGNED FEMALE/MALE AT BIRTH: when a baby is born and the doctor says, "It's a boy!" or, "It's a girl!" Usually this has to do with whether the doctor thinks the baby has a penis or a vagina. But even if it is unclear, the doctor will often assign the baby to one of these two categories.

BISEXUAL: attracted to people who are the same gender as you as well as people who are not

CHOSEN FAMILY: anyone a person comes to have a strong bond with and treats as family. Chosen family is extra important to many LGBTQ+ people because they have a greater chance of being rejected by the family they grew up with.

CHOSEN NAME: the name someone wants other people to call them

COME OUT: when a person chooses to tell someone else that they are LGBTQ+

CONVERSION THERAPY: a way people try to change someone else's sexual orientation or gender identity, often against their will

DISCRIMINATION: the unfair treatment of a group of people because of who they are

DRAG (KING/QUEEN): a person who performs in an exaggerated version of a particular gender regardless of their own gender

DRAG BALL/BALLROOM: drag competitions most commonly found in communities of color

DRAG MOTHER: an experienced drag queen who mentors or teaches newer performers

GAY: attracted to people who are the same gender. It can be used for anyone, but sometimes it is used specifically for a man who is attracted to other men.

GENDER-AFFIRMING: emotional, social, or medical support that makes a person feel more comfortable with their gender

GENDER MARKER: a place, usually on an official document like a passport or driver's license, where a person's gender is indicated. Often it is the letter M for "male," the letter F for "female," or an X for anything else.

GENDER-NEUTRAL: not emphasizing any gender over others

GENDER-NONCONFORMING: having traits that don't fit into others' expectations of "male" or "female"

GENDERQUEER: see *gender-nonconforming*

HARLEM RENAISSANCE: the flourishing of arts and culture during the 1920s and 1930s in Harlem, a historically Black neighborhood in New York City.

HIV/AIDS: HIV is a virus that makes people able to get the disease AIDS, which is characterized by the body's immune system attacking itself. Many LGBTQ+ people died from AIDS in the 1980s and 1990s before treatments were developed.

HOMOPHOBIA: dislike or hatred of someone because they are gay, bisexual, or lesbian

HOMOSEXUAL: attracted to people who are the same sex

IN THE CLOSET: living in a way that hides a person's sexuality or gender identity

LESBIAN: a woman who is attracted to other women

LGBTQ+: Lesbian, Gay, Bi(sexual), Trans, Queer/Questioning, and others. This acronym is commonly used to refer to a wide range of people who have faced prejudices based on their gender or sexual orientation.

MISGENDER: incorrectly assume the gender of someone else

NONBINARY: neither male or female in gender

PRIDE: a celebration by and for LGBTQ+ people that usually takes place in June

PRONOUNS: words that stand in for people's names when talking about them, like "This is my friend Alex. **She** is from Kansas, and this is **her** cat!" The most used pronouns are she/her, he/him, and they/them.

QUEER: having an LGBTQ+ identity. In the past, this was used as an insult, but now many LGBTQ+ people use it for themselves as a way to reclaim the term and take away its negative power.

RACISM: discrimination against someone of a different race based on the belief that one's own race is superior

SEXIST: prejudiced because of gender, usually against women

SEXUAL ORIENTATION: who you're attracted to

SOCIAL JUSTICE: the act of making wealth, opportunities, and privileges within a society more fair and equal for everyone

STONEWALL REBELLION: a series of riots and demonstrations that sparked when police raided a gay bar in New York City called the Stonewall Inn in June of 1969. These demonstrations helped inspire an international fight for LGBTQ+ rights.

TOMBOY: someone people see as a girl who doesn't act girly enough

TOP SURGERY: an operation on the top half of the body, usually involving either having breasts removed or breast implants put in.

TRANSGENDER (TRANS): someone whose gender is different from the gender they were assigned at birth

TRANSITION: any number of things a person does to make themself feel more comfortable and secure in their gender identity. This can include things like changing their name, taking hormones, getting surgery, or changing what clothes they wear.

TRANSVESTITE: someone who wears clothing that most people think belongs to another gender

TWO-SPIRIT: a term used by Indigenous Peoples belonging to several Native Nations who have long recognized more than two genders.

VISIBILITY: the act of deliberately drawing attention to LGBTQ+ people and their accomplishments because so often they have been ignored

RESOURCES

Black Lives Matter Foundation (blacklivesmatter.com): organization for Black equality, including Black LGBTQ+ equality

COLAGE (colage.org): organization for children of LGBTQ+ parents

Family Equality Council (familyequality.org): advocates for LGBTQ+ families

GLAAD (www.glaad.org): Gay and Lesbian Alliance Against Defamation

GLSEN (www.glsen.org): Gay, Lesbian & Straight Education Network

GSA Network (gsanetwork.org): helps LGBTQ+ youth create alliances to fight homophobia and transphobia in schools

Human Rights Campaign (hrc.org): LGBTQ+ legal advocacy group

It Gets Better Project (itgetsbetter.org): resources to help empower LGBTQ+ youth

National LGBTQ Task Force (thetaskforce.org): LGBTQ+ movement organization since 1973

PFLAG (www.pflag.org): Parents and Friends of Lesbians and Gays

The Trevor Project (www.thetrevorproject.org): provides mental health support to LGBTQ+ youth

EXPLORE MORE LINKS!

"Anomalies: Venom Race" on YouTube: https://www.youtube.com/watch?v=WzuggJbWfRs&t=12s

Britannica Kids article on the U.S. government: https://kids.britannica.com/kids/article/United-States-Government/353887

Google Doodle inspired by Willi Ninja: https://www.youtube.com/watch?v=SCN8iYJdfGU

"Harlem: A Dream Deferred" from *A Raisin in the Sun*: https://www.youtube.com/watch?v=v6JXHzyX60M

"How Does the Brain Help us Understand Others?" on *Frontiers for Young Minds*: https://kids.frontiersin.org/articles/10.3389/frym.2022.760058

Lammy-winning books from Lambda Literary Foundation: https://lambdaliterary.org/awards/lammys-directory-1988-present/

Nickelodeon Kids' Choice Awards: https://www.nick.com/kids-choice-awards

Operation Ouch video on how X-rays work: https://www.youtube.com/watch?v=3uC21wfeDol

Oscar Wilde Memorial Bookshop: https://www.nyclgbtsites.org/site/oscar-wilde-memorial-bookshop/

OutSchool comedy classes: https://outschool.com/online-classes/comedy

"The Power of Yet" for *Sesame Street*: https://www.youtube.com/watch?v=XLeUvZvuvAs&t=4s

"What Are Unions and How Do They Work?" on YouTube: https://www.youtube.com/watch?v=aI5N_5TvFOA

"What Is Media Literacy?" on YouTube: https://www.youtube.com/watch?v=GIaRw5R6Da4

ACKNOWLEDGMENTS

I would like to thank my editor, the brilliant Kristen Depken, for coming up with an ambitious series of deadlines and providing great support along the way. Thanks to Katie Cicatelli-Kuc for convincing me this was something I could do in the first place. Sarah Miller and Luca Brassi, you are my home and my light. I would be nothing without my communities of support: The Brooklyn Gay Wizards, the Simone de Beauvoir Distinguished Women's Circle, the PVD CrossFit Queers, the Hestons of Delaware and Ohio, the Sadlers, and the Millers. For providing help and encouragement along the way: Thank you Nico Medina, Billy Merrell, Sylvia Warren, Samantha Butler, and Louisa Mandarino. And, finally, thank you to my nephew David, who kept insisting I put myself in this book based solely on the title.

ABOUT THE AUTHOR

L. V. Heston is an editorial manager at Oxford University Press. They received a PhD in sociology for their study of LGBTQ+ chosen family forms from the University of Massachusetts, Amherst. They currently live in Providence, Rhode Island, with their dazzling wife and handsome cat. This is their first book.

Helder Oliveira is a self-taught illustrator from the Amazonian region of Brazil. Although he earned his degree in physiotherapy, he decided to shift careers to illustration in 2017. Since then, Helder has worked for clients all over the globe. He currently lives in São Paulo.

www.ingramcontent.com/pod-product-compliance
Lightning Source LLC
Chambersburg PA
CBHW060859090426
42737CB00024B/3490